# Let the First Rep Suck

Todd Bumgardner, MS

Copyright ©2019, Todd Bumgardner, MS

All rights reserved. It is not legal to reproduce, duplicate, or transmit any part of this document in either electronic means or printed format. Recording of this publication is strictly prohibited.

ISBN: 978-0-578-61584-4

*Some call you Special K, others call you Hot Kath, I call you mom. If it weren't for your steadfastness, dedication, toughness, and love, I'd probably be dead in a ditch somewhere. This wouldn't exist without you. Thank you, mom.*

# Contents

Forewords ................................................... 7
Preface ....................................................... 13
Introduction ................................................ 21
Why People Want A Coach ........................... 33

**Part I: The Three Pillars of Fitness Coaching** 53

    Pillar I: Psychological Safety ........................... 57
    Pillar II: Guidance ......................................... 137
    Pillar III: Aims and Goals .............................. 237

**Part II: Managing the Three Fitness Coaching Environments** ............................................. 303

    Small Group Personal Training ..................... 305
    One-on-One Personal Training ..................... 315
    Group Training ............................................ 327

**Concluding Thoughts** ................................. 341
**Acknowledgements** ................................... 345
**About the Author** ...................................... 347

# Forewords

Over the last 20 years, I've developed the ability to identify golden resources in the fitness and performance world. If you are reading this I believe you are holding one of those resources in your hands. I can say that with certainty because I know the guy who wrote it.
Many years ago, I stumbled on this guy Todd "The Red Rocket" Bumgardner while reading on a popular website. I had no idea who he was as a person or a coach, but I liked his writing style and the information he was sharing. Fast forward a decade or so and I call Todd a real friend and still love reading his work and insights. He's one of my go to resources on all things coaching and human development. His mind is unique, his ability to communicate complex messages in simple terms is incredible and he's as committed as anyone to making this industry better.

Reading this book will give you access to Todd's brain and perspective on coaching. It will most likely make you question your own as well. Which in my experience, is a good thing. I'm excited to get this book in the hands of my team and staff so we can steal all the gold and knowledge shared within the coming pages....and you'd be a fool not to do the same.

Todd is one of the leaders in education in our industry and after reading this you will know exactly why.

## Andy McCloy
July, 2019

I don't remember the exact moment I became award of Todd.

I think it was from an article on T-nation that he wrote. I found out soon after that he was the training partner of our mutual friend, Dr. Mike Roussell. Dr. Mike had mentioned in passing that Todd was a good human and that we should meet.

I, of course, ignored his recommendation at the time. My mistake number one.

Fast forward to a Strength Faction seminar where I was invited to speak and teach.

I was set up for Day 2, but I sat in on Day 1.

I was hanging out with Todd prior to his talk. He was very casual. Unafraid to be himself. He was funny, friendly, and inquisitive. He cursed frequently.

His behavior lets you relax and be yourself. You like him right away. But I didn't think he'd talk about anything in depth that would impress me.

My mistake number two.

He didn't talk sets and reps, assessment, or anything that most would consider at a fitness and training seminar.

He spoke of how to develop the human first. Not your typical subject for a meathead trainer. It turns out that Todd has studied what it means to be human at a very deep level. (My first gift from Todd included books from Carl Jung and Jordan Peterson. Not the typical offering in the fitness industry, but quite possibly, more useful than books about sets and reps.)

At this point in my career, I rarely took a lot of notes at fitness seminars, but I was immediately inspired and began filling my notebook as Todd spoke. From his talk, my personal and professional philosophy evolved in that moment, and I wrote it down.

Since that seminar, I've had the opportunity to get to know Todd pretty well. He's now on the favorite humans list.

I get to read his writing before most others. I get to listen to the songs he writes on his guitar before everyone on social media.

What I've learned is that Todd's understanding of you begins with his attempts to understanding of himself.

He has questions like we all do, but he's got a superpower of self-awareness that is essential for a coach and a teacher to understand his clients and his pupils.

What you are about to invest in by reading this book is your opportunity to learn in depth how to help others succeed.

You'll learn it within a context that is simple and comfortable for you whether you're the coach, the trainer, or the therapist.

What I think is even more impactful is that you'll get to borrow and develop Todd's superpower of self-awareness and understanding to help you become the best version of yourself.


**Bill Hartman**
November 20, 2019

# Preface

During my junior year of high school, I had the roughest football practice of my entire career. It was special teams practice, and we were covering our responsibilities on that fourth down scenario that every offensive coach tries to avoid—the punt. Along with being the starting, right-side outside linebacker, I was also the up-back on the punt team...among other things. When you play for a moderately-sized high school in Central Pennsylvania, and you're a good athlete, you have to do more than one job.

As the up-back, I'd have to scan the opposing punt return team, decide if they were going to rush hard to block the punt, determine our blocking and coverage scheme, and then make a call to my teammates so everyone was on the same page and doing the right job. The blocking scheme we were practicing accounted for a hard, middle rush—a linebacker from the opposing team would sprint through the A-gap, that's the one between the center/snapper and the guard, in order to disrupt or block the punt. That lunatic was my responsibility.

And the kid playing that linebacker role in practice that day was kind of a lunatic. His name was Nick, well it probably still is, I think he's still alive, and he had the biggest head of any human I'd ever seen. Seriously, they had to special order this kid's helmet. He was also about 225 pounds to my 185, and he really, really liked to hit things—and by things I definitely mean people. His job on that day was to challenge my ability to manage that linebacker during a hard, middle rush. The team we'd be playing that Friday night had a similar lunatic-type person, and I'd have to hand him his ass should he decide to come through that A-gap.

While doing my best to avoid sounding like some uber-macho douche canoe, I'll say that I've never shied away from contact. I think it's fun. My football career was littered with instances of me getting in trouble because I decided to run into someone when I had the opportunity not to—whether that was knocking a receiver off of his feet instead of going for an interception or lowering my shoulder on a defender as I carried the ball rather than making a move and getting into the open field. But on the day that Nick and I had to tango in the A-gap during punt practice, my head wasn't right—and on our first meeting in the hole he drove me back nearly into the punter.

As I made my way forward to meet him, I saw his eyes spread wide, almost, it seemed, taking up the gigantic mass that was called his head (I need you to appreciate how big this human's head is), and I immediately knew I was in trouble. I knew I didn't go as hard as I should have, and the smarter Todd that lives inside my brain said, "You're toast. Nice going." Then, as I came to this realization, I tried to turn it on. But it was too late. Nick drove me back ten yards and my coach, the legendary Gawen Stoker, was on my ass right-quick and in a hurry.

Two paragraphs ago, I mentioned that my "head wasn't right" on that fateful day of my ass whooping. The year before, my dad left my mom and I, and family life since that day had been a tumult of change and emotion. My mom and I (her street name is Hot Kath) had to leave our house and move into a small, double-wide trailer close to my high school. She still lives there today, doing her daily exercises, taking walks and drinking decaf coffee with her friends—her neurologist advises against caffeine since Hot Kath had a stroke back in 2014. There was an immense amount of financial stress and uncertainty. My mother had lost a marriage, and she had to deal with that while also continuing to work and keep us afloat. I never, truly thought a ton of my dad, he didn't give me a lot of reasons to, but I at least thought he cared. And now, he was gone. That took a while to settle in for me.

The night he left came during the summer before my sophomore year of high school, and for some reason, it didn't affect me as much on the field during that season. I was this cocky shit that thought he could rule the world, and I played like it. I played well. But as my junior year came around, the cumulative effect settled in, and while I still played well, I started the entire season at outside linebacker on a state playoff qualifying team, my head would get the best of me at times. My focus wasn't at its usual intensity and my confidence frequently failed me. I'd gone from being a sophomore with enough swagger to share with the entire county to a junior that was skating by on talent and glimpses of brilliance by making big plays to save my starting position.

Coach Stoker obviously saw the change. And, as it goes in small, rural communities, he had to have known about my dad leaving—even though I never said a word about it to him. Some false sense of toughness, fear on masquerade, kept my mouth shut when I should have talked to someone that I knew cared deeply about me. I was also a kid...and being a kid in that situation isn't easy. But, none-the-less, looking back as a grown man, I'm certain that he knew.

He flew on to the field after the first snap during which Nick made me his sad, little play thing and yelled, "Bummy, what the hell was that?" (Bummy is the unfortunate nickname you get when your last name is Bumgardner and you live in Central Pennsylvania.) I'm certain I replied with something like, "I don't know, coach." He made us line up and do it again. During the subsequent rep I improved, but Nick was still gave me the business. I did my job, and prevented him from disrupting the punt, but he still owned me.

"You're going to let him do that to you? You're going to let him push you around like that? Come on, Todd Bumgardner. Go. Hit. Him." After that second play, Coach Stoker laid something like that on me. He stood right in front of me, looked directly into my face and challenged me.

"Go hit him, Bummy."

He knew me, although at the time I didn't realize how well. He knew the chip I had on my shoulder, my natural aversion to being pushed around, my love of contact. He knew that my confidence had waned and that the rest of my life away from football was in flux. He knew that I needed to see that I could do something—that I could run into a 225-pound mass of human with an obnoxiously large head and stop that mass in place. Coach Stoker knew I needed to prove that to myself. It wasn't just about my job on punt team anymore.

We ran it again and I lined up a little closer to the line of scrimmage, eyes a bit narrower, confidence returning, and a little angry—angry that I got pushed around, and angry with myself for letting it happen. As soon as I called the cadence, and the ball left the snapper's hands, I met Nick in the A-gap with everything my 185-pound frame had, my feet driving, my helmet lower than his trying to drive him skyward, our bodies jolted as we smashed them into each other. We were locked in a stalemate. He couldn't move me back. I stopped him in his tracks.

I hit him.

Gawen Stoker knew the team needed me to perform—to do my job. But he also knew me, and he knew I needed to be challenged. Coach knew who I was, what words would tempt my mettle into showing itself, what my personality needed so that my eyes would narrow, and I'd throw myself forward. He knew I needed to get my confidence back, and he gave a 16-year old kid the opportunity to be something more than he currently was.

That's the torch we all still have to carry as coaches. The one that illuminates who our people are and what they currently need from us. It gives us the vision to create the environment that people can meet the stronger versions of themselves that's waiting for them on the other side of their transformation.

I obviously didn't know it at the time, but I think that's when I started to write this book. Maybe it was the cumulative effect, the collection of moments with Coach Stoker, and the other people that deeply influenced me, that, nearly two decades ago, penned the first words in my recollection.

It began with wanting to be a teacher that was also the head football coach—something I was modeling, although unconsciously, from Coach Stoker. But as life carried on and my interests and priorities changed, I ended up in the fitness-coaching world (even though I did a short stint as a football coach). What I started learning from my favorite coach over a few falls during the early 2000s has only grown into a greater drive to help other people develop and challenge themselves. And now here we are.

This book is my gift back to coaching and training—the two gifts given to me that forged the bigger parts of who I am. I've dedicated my entire adult life to better understanding people, the complexities of their mental and emotional lives (as well as their bodies), and I've worked hard to condense all that I've learned into a simple, actionable coaching philosophy. That's what I'm presenting to you in this work.

I hope it serves you well in your journey to grow as a coach and a person. Here's to carrying the torch forward that Coach Stoker lit for me.

# Introduction

## Some Things Up Front

Let's level on something before we carry the discussion forward and add fuel to the proverbial torch we're carrying.

*I'm not just going to spoon-feed you information.*

It's totally against my educational philosophy—answers achieved easily, or without context, rarely do the appropriate good. They don't resonate with staying power. While I'm going to use this book to help you improve at your craft and give you some answers, you're going to have to work for them—hard-earned lessons create the better parts of who we are.

While I don't know that the material in this book is an inherent intellectual challenge, I'm challenging you to read it in a challenging way. Read it with the context of the coaching problems that you're currently trying to solve, read it as if you're mining for the raw materials you currently need to improve your coaching. I can't tell you what that is, and hell, you might not be totally conscious of it right now either.

But I promise you that it's in there; reading just might illuminate it. And if you read as if you're mining for the stuff you need to solve that problem, you'll be able to apply the philosophy, the stories, and the action items from this book in your own practice. You'll get better.

As an example, let's say that you're having a difficult time with "client compliance." I use the quotations because compliance has an air of dictatorial and directive, and I don't think that's what we do. But it's a common term that I know will be understood. So, let's say folks aren't following the fitness path you're laying out for them. They're not getting the results that you, or they, would like, and you're not sure what to do about it. Read these pages looking for the answer.

Take a few minutes to brainstorm all of the coaching questions you're currently trying to answer—or just the aspects of your coaching that you're trying to improve. Once you've got your list, consult it each time before you crack this book open. Scour the pages, using your self-provided context, for the answers.

I challenge you to do this for the rest of your life. Read every book as if it were written for you and the current place that you're in. The things that you're thinking about, the problems that you're trying to solve, the answers that you need—they are subjectively contained somewhere in the information that you're consuming. Remaining distant from the material and reading as a cold, objective observer rarely gives us what we need. We have to read subjectively. We read while considering our current personal and professional standing. Without that consideration it's difficult to extract the information we want, and need, in a context that's useful to us. True engagement requires subjectivity. Read for you.

I'm not, however, recommending blind acceptance of what you read—even as it pertains to this book. I'm certainly not perfect and my ideas aren't gospel. Reading for you also means reading with a critical eye and in an effort to generate questions. As you read, think of your current situation(s), the problems you're trying to solve, but also try to punch holes in what I'm saying. Use your experience and weigh it against what I'm saying. Take the information that I'm sharing to your work and decide whether or not it fits for you.

I promise, even as I'm asking you to read in a challenging way, that you're going to find directly applicable information in this book that is going to immediately impact the way that you coach. Commit yourself to working through the information, asking questions about it, trying it out, taking notes, and deciding for yourself what is going to stick for you. Then, use it to build, or improve, your own coaching philosophies and systems.

# What You're Going to Get Out of This

While my instructions are for you to *read this book for you*, directing what you're going to get it out of it toward a purposefully-aimed high level of subjectivity, there are specific, concrete things I'm giving to you.

You're going to get exactly what I do, and what I teach our coaches to do, on a day-to-day basis. This book is going to answer questions like, "How do I get clients to buy into my coaching on the floor?" "What do I do to help clients set goals?" "What actually brings clients into the gym and how can that understanding help me as a coach?" "How do I manage different fitness coaching environments?" You may not see those questions specifically posed, but this sucker is going to answer them. For the remainder of this section, we'll walk through the different sections of the book, how they flow, and how they'll work to answer questions like the ones above.

We get the party started by getting into the nitty gritty of what fitness coaching is and why people seek it out. We'll apply that understanding as we party on throughout the rest of the book.

Psychological safety breaks down the two environments we manage as fitness coaches—the interpersonal and the physical. We'll have a discussion on the basics of the environments and how to construct a healthy one

of each. Included in the discussion on the interpersonal environment are tools that helps us illuminate
the differences in personalities, how practicing unconditional positive regard lays a healthy foundation for a productive interpersonal environment, and tools for managing yourself for so that you can be the coach your clients need you to be.

Moving on to the physical environment, we'll talk about consistency, order, and ritual and how the sum of the elements of a good physical environment far exceeds the individual parts.

Guidance is the absolute crux of what we do, and this section talks about the what, why, and how associated with successfully guiding a client from point A to B and beyond. Step number one is actually remembering that we are the guide and not the hero—the Obi Wan to our clients' Luke Skywalker. We'll move on to the actions that will help you improve your everyday, on-the-floor coaching. You'll learn about a coaching paradigm that's successfully coached thousands of people that leads into the ins and outs of cueing. And we'll have a discussion on accountability and what it really is.

Over the years, I've found that the toughest part of most folks' training journey is articulating and acting on goals. People struggle with putting into words exactly what they want to do and how they are going to do it. Mostly, it seems the people aren't good at it because they haven't done it all that often. Goal setting, like anything else, is a skill to be cultivated. In the section on Aims and Goals, I lay out the process we use to help our clients articulate their actual desires and also get good and stating them and approaching them with their actions.

We'll close this party out with discussions on managing the three common training environments—personal training, small-group personal training, and group training. I lay out productive ways to construct these training environments. And when I say productive I mean easy for you to manage and results-driven for your clients.

Then, on your way out the door, I'll hand you a parting gift of concluding thoughts.

After years and years of work, I'm excited to share these ideas with you. To give you a bit more context and clarity before jumping in to our main discussions, I'm outlining the life-cycle of a client at BSP NOVA in non-fiction story form. It'll give you the 30,000 foot view before diving in to learn the constituent parts and actions that we've melded together to create a consistently world-class coaching product. From this perspective, you'll be able to draw more from the practical, as well as the philosophical, discussions we're about to have.

# The Lifecycle of a Client

Harry likes to party, but it makes sense. He's a single dude in his 30s that frequents the recreational softball and baseball leagues—playing on multiple teams several nights of the week from the spring through the fall. As much as the rec leagues are designed to keep folks playing beloved childhood games, they're equally purposed for social interaction. And that usually means tossing a few brews back during every game. Those brews that find their way down the hatch have a funny way of directing a lady or gent to a bar after the game to continue the fun.

Our guy Harry (a real client at BSP NOVA with a currently fictionalized name) makes no bones about it—he loves to play softball, to play baseball, and to drink. Those things are meaningful to him and he's not showing them the door anytime soon. At least not completely—he's compromised on the amount of each in the name of his health and his goals. But, nonetheless, Harry's been real with us about that since he first sat down with us for a 1-on-1 Assessment and Goal-Setting session. He came to us wanting to work hard, wanting to lose weight, wanting to get stronger and improve his performance, but not wanting to totally give up the things he loves doing.

While there are many courses of action we could have taken in trying to support Harry, two stand out as the most plausible: *lean on him hard to change his lifestyle and give him a big dose of finger wagging, or meet him where he was at and get on the same page about his current capacity and what he was willing to do.* We, as we do with all of our clients, chose the latter option. It seemed to work out pretty well. In less than a year, Harry dropped from over 210 pounds to the 160s while continuing to play the bat sports he so loves and keeping his social life intact. How was Harry able to drop the pounds while still smacking softballs and sinking suds? We had a consistent, honest dialogue that helped make it easier for him to choose to do the work.

Consistent, honest dialogue is the centering principle of the life-cycle of a client at our gym. From introduction, to goals-achieved and beyond, the process is based on a continuing conversation that places the client, their wants, their needs, and their willingness to act in the forefront. This book covers, in the greatest detail that I'm capable of, just how we use that process to keep that dialogue rolling in each of our coaching settings—small-group personal training, group training, and personal training. We'll talk about all of this in detail in different parts of the book, but I thought a brief overview of how things actually work at our gym would provide context that improves your understanding as you read.

It starts with our 1-on-1 Assessment and Goal-Setting session—the initial consultation that we do with every new small group personal training client that starts at our gym. The goal of this session is learning. We learn as much about them as we possibly can, and we give them the opportunity to learn as much as possible about us while helping them find the training solution that's right for them—be it small-group personal training, group training, or personal training. This session was the first time we learned about Harry's love of recreational sports and his love of being social, and how we could best help him without declaratively dogging the other important aspects of his life.

The 1-on-1 Assessment and Goal-Setting session sets the initial course toward helping the client accomplishing their goals while also demonstrating in a big way that we actually care and want to listen to what they have to say. We'll talk about this session in detail in the section on aims and goals.

At the end of their initial consultation, a new client schedules their Personal Orientation session. During this session the client gets introduced to our small-group personal training approach. Rather than giving them a kick to the keister and saying, "Good luck!" and immediately jumping them onto an individualized program, we teach them the warm-up, the basic movements that we use, and give them as much education as we possibly can on how things work in our environment. For us, it's another opportunity to see them move, learn about their personality, and gather other general information we can share with the rest of the coaching team. We get a clearer picture on where to start with their program design and how to best fit our coaching to them. At the completion of this session they schedule their first small group personal training session.

At this point, the client begins their individualized training program. The information gathered from the 1-on-1 Assessment and Goal-Setting session and their Personal Orientation session is synthesized to create a high level of customization. They are, of course, closely instructed on how to perform all of the exercises on their program, but they're given some more free reign to move about the gym while still under our watchful, guiding eye. This is when we start introducing folks to GAB, a goal-setting tool we borrowed from Motivational Interviewing—something you'll learn about during the section on guidance. Throughout the course of a program we use GAB to help folks focus in on the task at hand and have productive training sessions.

Within this meta-structure of dialogue there is the day-to-day, on-the-floor art of coaching movement. The masterpiece of this medium is consistently putting an individual in the best positions to be successful based on their movement competencies and capacities—then watching them grow stronger and more capable with each passing training session. We are forever dedicated to improving our on-the-floor coaching, and up to now we've created a coaching process that is easy for our coaches to apply and easy for our clients to reap the benefits of. The result is a lot of folks training hard in positions that fit their bodies and getting constant results because of it—the driving force of the client life-cycle.

If all goes to plan, a client finishes their program in four to six weeks—depending on their membership and how many times per week they're training. Then it's time for what we call an EoP. It's an End of Phase chat. When clients, old and new, finish a training program they fill out a questionnaire on the back of their program and have a quick sit-down with a coach. During the convo—the continuation of that dialogue started during their initial consultation—the client and the coach recap what went well, and didn't go so well, during the previous program as they set their sights on the next program's priorities, goals, and actions. The EoP Process gets repeated three more times until they finish a "block" of training—which in BSP NOVA world is four programs. Then it's time for some longer-term planning using our End of Block meeting.

The dialogue continues with a larger scope. Client and coach work together to project further into the future and take on bigger aspirations than can be accomplished during one training program. But rather than jumping in with a conversation, our EoB process begins with internal dialogue. We send the client home with a form to fill out so that they can think about their goals, what the think they can do to achieve them, and the beginnings of an action plan. Then, armed with their thoughts and their writing, the client sits down with a coach to flush out the details—helping to give the goals as much defined shape as possible while also defining the actions that will transform the goals into a future reality.

This process, minus the 1-on-1 Assessment and Goal-Setting session which is one-time deal, continues on ad infinitum for as long as the person is a BSP NOVA client. It works for people because it meets them where they are at while beginning, and sustaining, a conversation that supports them with consistent guidance that is direction-giving and skill-building. It's the process that allowed Harry to make so many positive changes in his life while still smashing softballs and tossing a few back each week—and it's worked for many other clients in a way that's form-fitted to their lives while also providing the necessary consistent structure.

The meta-structure of the life-cycle, the day-to-day cueing, the relationship building we do with clients, it all begins with, and is guided by, a foundational philosophy—an understanding of what fitness coaching is and why people seek it out. Let's talk about that.

# Why People Want A Coach

## What Is A Fitness Coach?
## (Some Folks Call Us Personal Trainers, Strength Coaches, etc.)

A fitness coach, in a metaphorical way of speaking, serves as a client's training GPS. We help folks figure out where they currently are in their training journey and then plot a course toward the destination they'd like to reach. There's a great deal of repositioning back on course as some plans don't work and alluring detours lead them astray. Fitness coaching is guiding clients forward from plan to plan. And when a plan doesn't work, it's being there to help them craft the next one—all while putting them in the best positions possible to be successful from a movement standpoint—as well as a psychological and environmental one.

To give the above metaphor a lens of practicality, here's the working definition of coaching that I've used for the past five years:

> "Inciting the right interventions and challenges at the right times, based on personality, current status, and goals, to help a person, or group of people, to progress toward a desired outcome."

Keep in mind that this is my definition. It's not one that you'll find in a textbook or while perusing any peer-reviewed literature. That puppy is the outcome of years of study, observation, and implementation in a continuous cycle. It's the outcome of revamping my approach every time I've realized that I was wrong, that I learned something new, or that I just simply innovated a better way of using a coaching process. I'm positive that with time, attention, effort, and experience, this definition will evolve and likely become simpler. That's always the aim. But for now, it serves us well.

Fitness coaching, when rendered to its simplest form, is putting individuals in the best possible positions to be successful from all parameters that can be considered. The complexity of coaching exposes itself when we have to consider all of those parameters. People are outrageously complex. Our species is like a Rubix cube met the toughest calculus problem ever encountered and then gave birth to the theory of relativity. But then the theory of relativity got knocked up and birthed some crazy-asshole quantum mechanics problem. Yep, that's us—people. We're incredible, we're all a little crazy, and we're awesome. Most of all, we're here to help each other. Helping, especially from a coach's point of view, requires us to handle all of that complexity. Just how do we do that?

We do it with simple systems that help us to narrow our focus and broaden our understanding. These are the starting points that help us relate to people, get to know them, get to understand them, and ultimately be a catalyst that fuels their positive evolution.

We'll cover a bunch of these starting points and systems in this book, starting with a filtering framework that helps us understand just why it is that people seek out fitness coaching. Call me crazy, but I've found it much easier to work with a person, and help them ultimately progress in a way that they desire, if I have a basic understanding of why people seek me out in general. After that, specifics add detail to the picture.

There are three main reasons that people hire fitness coaches, and we'll talk about each in depth during their own section—to feel/gain competency, to change their self-perception, and to feel human connection.

*The Fitness Seeker's 3 Reasons for Coaching:*

1. *To Feel/Gain Competency*
2. *To Change Their Self-Perception*

## 3. To Feel Human Connection

## To Feel/Gain Competency

Humans have a natural need to feel competent. We innately want to understand the environments that we are in so that we can successfully navigate them. Navigation, in this sense, means understanding an environment well enough to relax, co-exist with others, know where we fit, and, extract what we need. Considering all of that, competency is a basic, primordial way to lower threat—keeping us emotionally stable. This is true for our self-perception as well as our social interactions. The two are locked in a never-ending, cyclically influential relationship—our individual state of affairs affecting our social state of affairs and vice versa. We want to feel safe, we want to feel social acceptance, and we want to act with a brave forthrightness that garners our self-respect. Feelings of competence help to regulate the entire, complex interaction.

Personality, innate ability, and past experiences all influence how we measure our own competence. To illustrate, let's look at an example based mostly on personality. Introverts that also deal with social anxiety often have a rough time at a bar or a party with a lot of noise and social interaction. As they walk in, maybe they think, "Son of a bitch, how can I look distracted so that I don't have to actually talk to anyone? Oh, look! There's a life-sized painting of Andy Dick. I'll go pretend to be super interested." And it works until someone notices them noticing and then the plot is foiled! Gasp! Then the stress sets in and they, with a little help from a self-fulfilling prophecy, end up saying, or doing, something that they think is silly because the situation pushes them past their capacity to competently navigate that environment.

Beyond preferring quiet and alone time, introverts with anxiety often don't have a good strategy for social situations to mitigate the overwhelm they feel from conversation and outward expression of energy. But if an anxious introvert had a plan for the party, maybe a strategy that systematically exposed him or her to more conversations before being thrust into the chaos of extroverts chattering, they'd likely feel more comfortable, more competent, when that person inevitably interrupted an attempt to hide in the splendor of Andy Dick's face. And maybe, just maybe, they'd actually have the confidence and composure to approach someone else at the party and talk to them first.

The same is true for extroverts, only in reverse. If there's not movement, conversation, or people around they aren't sure what to do with themselves. Sitting quietly is cruel and unusual punishment that stretches the bounds of their affective regulation. So, they give themselves a distraction—sometimes any distraction will do. But, if they had a strategy that made them feel competent in navigating a quiet, solitary environment, there's a solid chance that their emotions wouldn't be stretched in such a profound way.

I'm using these extremes as illustrations. If we, as human-person-beings, don't feel competent in navigating an environment we can't regulate our affective world. That means we can't effectively direct our actions—we get overwhelmed emotionally and, at the most practical level, we just don't know what to do. Not knowing what to do is de-motivating. If people feel inept, it's likely that they'll shy away from the thing, or the environment, that's making them feel that way. That's why it is so important to help clients new to the gym, or at least new to you, to feel competent early and often as they begin training with you.

Socially, competence is safe. (Heads up: the following is a logical, but conjectural, argument. It's a solid illustration, but I'm not an anthropologist. I'm just using an idea to make something make sense based on what I've learned, and what I've witnessed, in the life and times of being Todd Bumgardner.) Not only are we social beings, we're innately tribal—as demonstrated by fanatical violence felt, and demonstrated, when a professional football team "greets" fans from another major U.S. City. Philadelphia, we're all looking at you. Being tribal, the survival of the group depends on the strength of the individuals in it—so, being competent, by whatever measure that's deemed necessary by the given social group, is safe. Those that can't demonstrate competence are more likely to be cast-out, ostracized, and de-valued. This is, of course, dependent on culture. But valuing someone's ability to carry their own weight and provide is observably human.

Demonstrating that we can provide value, whether our skills are complimentary or competitive with others in the group, earns us a place at the table. And, at the most basic level, that place at the table matters to us...a lot. People, I'm not speaking of individuals right now but of the collective, structure the world so that we don't get affectively overwhelmed—a theme that keeps popping up in all of this competence talk. A lot of what we do is focused on understanding, managing, and manipulating our environments so that we aren't locked into a perpetual state of alarm. The funny paradox is that modern society, and the way we've decided to stress ourselves out, goes against its goal. But that place at the table, that feeling of being competent enough for the group to keep us around, that's, through my observation and reading, a serious drive for people across the board—though it's obviously not the only drive. The idea of competence is different from group to group, and the demonstration of it gets skewed, but, and this is reliant on mental health, we still want people to perceive us as able.

Where does all this talk fit into coaching? Well, understanding that people have innate drives, at several dynamic levels, to feel as though they are competent enough to handle an environment gives us the opportunity to structure our coaching, and our environment to help people meet that need. Initially, folks are outsourcing competence to us. They know that we know more about how to exercise, and they're leaning on our knowledge rather than spending *a bajillion hours* getting all of the answers. But, as time goes on, they're also extracting competency from us as they learn more and more about training. When we meet these needs, we deeply affect people and open the door for further connection—the connection needed for the foundation of a great client-coach relationship. We must, however, meet people at their current level of competency so that they can express it, grow in confidence and self-efficacy, and feel stable/safe enough to seek out challenges. And that, as we further the discussion in this here book, we'll see is one of the main objectives of our coaching. Something beautiful happens when that drive to take on challenges expands beyond the gym walls.

When I trained high school and college athletes out of a small, hole-in-the-wall gym in Central Pennsylvania, most of the kids that I worked with were male rugby and football players. Most of them were strapping, studly kinds of kids—tall, broad shoulders, you know the type. One of the football players introduced one of his non-football playing friends to the gym. To keep him anonymous, we'll make a fake name for him. Let's call him Fernando. Fernando and the football player were long-time family friends.

Fernando didn't look like the rest of the kids that trained in the gym. While he was relatively tall, he was also of much slighter build and, while the other hooligans played contact sports, he preferred band, track, and hanging out at the fire hall—a traditional Central Pennsylvania pastime. One of these things was not like the others, and in a lot of places a kid that wasn't like the majority of the others wouldn't have been so readily accepted. In our tiny, little corner of gym heaven slapped into a decrepit old building, he was—immediately. That acceptance sent him the message that he had the social competence to be in that space, and that did wonders for helping him relax and join the crew in an environment that, with loud music, heavy weights, and less than pristine aesthetics, was a little intimidating from the start. He'd also never weight trained before.

Our man Fernando was a decent hurdler on the track, but he wanted to be better. He also wanted to fit his frame up with some denser muscles. He trained hard to do both of those things, but at first, he wasn't super social—even though the guys were all cool with him. As muscle started fill out his frame, he felt more comfortable with the lifts on his program, and his track performance started to improve, we could all see a marked change in Fernando. He talked more. He joked around more. He started doing weird dances that no one could explain. It was like the Bernie and the robot got together and were like, "Hey, want to make people shit themselves?"

About the time Fernando started coming out of his shell, he started mentioning this girl that he wanted to take to a dance. He kept talking about her, but he hadn't asked. So, of course, in typically dude fashion, we all goaded him on, "Come, on dude, you just have to do it!" In reality, every person, at some point in their life has felt the terror of facing rejection, but it's so easy for us all to just say, "Come, on, man, what's it matter if she says no?" Oh, it matters. It matters a pad-load, Chet.

Sincerely, we wanted the best for him, so we did keep encouraging him to ask her out. And, finally, one day he walked into the gym with an air about him. Something had changed. He had a smile on his face from ear to ear, and, walked with an observably different sense of self. So, we immediately jumped in on him about what was up. Finally, after some prodding and ribbing, it came out. He'd asked her to the dance! I asked, "Well, what did she say?" He smiled back at me and said, "She said no," and the smile stayed on his face. And, of course, we all fell about the place. But there's something huge in this— monumentally huge in the scope of someone's life.

Fernando gained competence that directly affected his confidence and self-efficacy. He harvested knowledge from me, and the other guys, and applied it in transforming his body. The social capital he raised as being "one of the guys" gave him an improved perception of his social standing. Feelings of competence in one arena of life gave him the bravery to approach another arena of life, one he didn't traditionally feel as competent in, and walk toward the chaos of potential rejection—he approached the thing that scared him.

Beyond the foundational understanding of why people want to feel competent, Fernando's story sums up the real work we do and why helping our clients foster feelings of competence is so important. It's because bravery can be extrapolated. That feeling of "I got this" earned through training can give people the psychological means to approach other difficult parts of their lives with self-trust and resiliency. Fernando is the perfect example.

Competence, meeting a person at their current level of it and helping them push it forward, matters. It's the absolute, most important thing we do as coaches. We help people live bigger lives. Competence becomes self-efficacy. Self-efficacy bolsters confidence. Confidence builds bravery.

Bravery can be extrapolated.

## To Change Their Self-Perception

We want to think well of ourselves and we have a natural drive to make things better. I'm not saying that most people are walking around in some kind of woeful, downtrodden state trying to figure out how to like themselves. But I am saying that people, even those with healthy self-conceptions, like to make things better for themselves and improve their self-perception. We like it when we see that we can change for the better, that our actions have a positive impact—when we demonstrate that we can handle more, learn something new, be the one people count on, etc. This is all, of course, individually dependent—not everyone wants to perceive themselves well in the same way. But we all, barring mental and emotional disturbance, want to have healthy self-perception.

Our friend Fernando from the section on competency is a perfect example. He didn't, from my knowledge of him, think poorly of himself or dislike himself, but his ability to grow in the gym, and express that growth on the track, gave him a change in self-perception that affected the rest of his life. His change in self-perception because of his training, and his connection with a positive training environment, gave him the means to express more of himself because he saw himself differently. Rather than being the kid that sits back and pines, his newfound confidence told him that he was the kid that takes the risk and asks the girl out. There are few things better in the world than a person finding a positive part of themselves that they didn't know existed and using to improve their life. It's why I do what I do—and I'd slap a crisp 100-dollar bill down that says you feel a lot like I do.

When people first wrap their hands around the cold steel of a barbell, or hit send on that email to inquire about coaching, it's because they want to do something that will improve their lives. We could stick with the surface-level explanation and constrain that decision to the physical realm of bodily improvement. You know, just becoming like super-hot. Which, of course, would include a change in self-perception. But most people, even if they aren't totally conscious of it, are more complex than that. We run deeper. That 'wanting to be super-hot isn't the full story. People are like ogres and onions—we have layers. I'm not saying it's our job to peel back everyone's layers, but it certainly helps to get a few off the surface so that we can help people project themselves forward into the future and connect their actions to that projection. Something we'll discuss in detail in later pages.

People are spending their money with us because they want to change. Those changes, depending on the person, come at different levels. It's true that many folks feeling as though they want the change aren't totally ready for it. But still an internal dialogue, nonetheless, persists—telling them that the current version of whom they are isn't enough. They'd like to be something more. That something more could just be someone with a leaner frame, and that's totally cool. Maybe he or she just wants to look in the mirror and see that shape they've been missing. That would be enough for them to carry on in life with a better self-concept.

Mostly, however, I've noticed that feelings of competence underlie a lot of the reasoning and the desire for a change in self-perception. People want to see themselves as capable, strong, and worthy. Building a strong and resilient body is a simple way to make that mental shift. As a person witnesses their body growing stronger, embodying the ideal of strength actually affects their mental and emotional capacity to think more of themselves.

Stowed away in the back corner of our gym there are two giant tractor tires—one weighing on the north side of 700 pounds, the other between 200 and 300 pounds. They stand there, with a quiet, beckoning taunt, calling to all those that haven't flipped them. For many of the folks at our gym, especially women, the tires have become a self-imposed rite of passage. Inevitably, one woman will see another flipping the tire and remark to a coach something like, "That's awesome that she can do that. I wish I could do that." And, our coaches will reply with something like,

"Well, you can." Then, the woman says something like, "You really think so?" Of course. We know so.

The inception of the idea "I will flip the tire" sends the person on a journey. I've sincerely had clients cast all other goals aside so that they could prepare to flip the tire. A few hundred pounds of rubber and metal morphs into a new form—it becomes a dragon that must be slain. And to slay a dragon of this sorts, your body moves beyond flesh, becoming a sword to be sharpened. The sharpening of that sword steadies the mind, and the journey forms the sword and the user into one powerful being. Then the day comes. The journeyer slays the dragon. The tire is flipped.

They have emerged triumphant over a beast that taunted them. They're no longer some mere mortal. They are a person that can flip the tire, a strong, capable force to be reckoned with.

And now they are different. And they see that.

## To Feel Human Connection

"My ultimate goal is to not need to come to your gym. I want to know that I can do this on my own, but I'm not sure that I want to leave. I just love this community so much and I don't know if I want to give that up."

A client that's walked a trying road said this to me. We were seated in the soft, pleather chairs (Value City Furniture, thank you for your comfort and affordability) at the end of the turf that stretches the length of the gym, having our End of Program chat. She had come to us knowing that without our guidance she would over-exercise and end up in a very dark place. But she also knew that being able to exercise on her own was a dragon that she needed to hunt down and slay. At this point, her vision for the future was conflicted.

At the time of this writing, she's still our client, and she's still planning on "not needing us anymore", but she illustrates well the third reason that people seek out fitness coaching—they want to be connected to another human or humans. We all want to go on a journey, and there are solitary parts of every path, but none of us truly wants to walk the whole way alone. In my life, I haven't met anyone that could do anything great all by themselves. Sure, it's cliched, but it's true.

We'll talk about "being the guide" a little farther down the road in this book, but now, as we talk about connection, is a great time to introduce the concept. People want to feel connected to a guide that they trust—it's part of that whole outsourcing competency thing. For some folks, that guide is in a book, a magazine, or a YouTube video. But for the folks that hire us, the folks that want a coach—they want a living, breathing human that they can count on. They want someone that will listen as they tell their story. Not just a guide with answers that they don't have, but someone that sees them and understands them. While the coach-client relationship isn't the most intimate relationship in either party's life, it still reaches to a depth that's reliant on trusting vulnerability. That depth gives us cause to share our true story. It's something we all want. Sharing our story with someone that we know will actually hear it, without judgment, and will help us author the next chapter in our growth—that's human connection.

But clients aren't only seeking a guide. They are, often times, seeking connection with other people that are also on a journey—and having a central locus of connection, like the same coach or training facility, makes the dissolution of separation all the stronger. I don't think people even necessarily need to "see themselves" in the other clients, although for some folks it certainly helps. But being surrounded by others that are close to the same wave length is something that we all seek. And, for some reason, in our current world, places that people exercise together have evolved to scratch that itch.

Not every gym, even those that offer small group personal training and group training, fosters that connection. But every gym would do well to connect their people in a meaningful, community-minded way...because people, whether conscious of it or not, are seeking it. Even though different people go about it in different ways, everyone wants to be seen. Everyone wants to feel understood. Our relationships with our clients, and the relationships we foster between clients, can accomplish both of those ends.

Maybe it's the shared purpose—even if two people in the same training facility with the same coaches don't share a completely mutual purpose, they can at least share in *having purpose.* And purpose, if it's strong and sustainable, inevitably leads to struggle—whether it's to get a first push-up or to just consistently show up at the gym—and shared struggle is one of the most bonding elements of the human experience. People want that. We're at our best as coaches when we give it to them.

That "it" looks something like sitting in a pleather chair and listening to another person's story, completely, truly, and genuinely wanting to help them write the next chapter. It's giving them the structure and the space to write that next chapter by empowering them with your regard for them without any need for justification.

That "it" is a place where people can share in struggle and purpose. It's folks getting to know each other beyond the gym because a mutual desire for transformation drew them into the same space—fostering friendships that evolve between people that would have never met under any other circumstances. People showing up at a gym to do things that the unwilling public would deem insane, or at the very least, unnecessary, all while offering a hand and a kind word, is some of the strongest evidence of human connection in our realm.

So, when people sit across from in you in that consultation chair for the first time, or when you encounter them on the gym floor, searching for the correct plate to solve their gym math equation, realize that connection is part of what they are seeking. Even those abs that a client tells you that they want, they're about connection. In some way, that six pack is going to open a door for them, one that connects them more favorably with themselves or removes a barrier to connecting with others in some way. People are coming to us for connection.

And we have to give it to them.

# Part I: The Three Pillars of Fitness Coaching

"Well, what am I actually doing?"

That's the question holding dominion at the forefront of everything I do to develop a communicable system. It's the impetus of examination that illuminates actions worth documenting and sharing.

Though we like to believe that we're consciously in control of our self-direction, we're not always totally aware, are we? We act during a day, doing what works, or what seems to work, and then we move on to the next day innately repeating our actions at some level of semi-consciousness. Somewhere, semi-subconsciously, there's a register noting the outcomes, noting what went well and what didn't and silently shaping our working behavior. One of the perks I get from developing a staff of coaches and interns, and also running a business that mentors other coaches, is that I'm required to be acutely aware of my coaching choices—at least in a reflective sense. I have to stop myself daily and echo that illuminating question:

*"What am I actually doing?"*

If I didn't have to teach, I could go on living in my own head just doing without total awareness of my efforts. While that wouldn't be optimal, it would definitely be feasible. The good news, however, is that I have to teach—every week of my life. So, rather than living, working, and coaching with a semi-conscious awareness, I keep myself in touch with daily awareness of my actions. Then I take what's actually happening, what I'm doing that's working, and put it into words that can be understood and replicated. (Hint: If you truly want to form your thoughts and carry them out strategically, write about and teach others the things that you do!)

During one of these bouts of reflective awareness I was working to answer the question, "What do fitness coaches actually do?" And, subsequently, "What is it that we need to do to be able to do that...what is it that we need to create to do that thing that fitness coaches do?" These are the things that tangle my brain for days on end. The outcome of this seemingly unrelenting tangle of questions is the Three Pillars of Fitness Coaching.

In my estimation, these are the three things that all good fitness coaches do to help their clients make progress. They provide a psychologically "safe" environment, they serve as a guide, and they help people project themselves forward, turning their wants and needs into aims and goals that can be planned and acted on. These three pillars give sturdiness to the fitness coach and his or her ability to be an agent of positive, transformational change.

*The Three Pillars of Fitness Coaching*

1. *Psychological Safety*
2. *Guidance*
3. *Aims and Goals*

Create an environment stocked with systems that erect these three pillars and your coaching will have a stable foundation that you can build on. The rest of this book, I do solemnly swear, will help you fashion the strongest coaching pillars seen since the time of Milo and that crazy bull he carried around on his shoulders.

In the name of gathering the raw materials to construct your coaching foundation, let's talk in depth about each pillar.

# Pillar I: Psychological Safety

Let's start this conversation with a seemingly contradictory declaration:

*The gym is not a safe place.*

How's that for psychological safety? At first glance, and without further explanation, you might think, "This Bumgardner fellow is a real jack-hole, and I'm not sure I fancy what he has to say." But let me explain that declaration and you might take back all that name calling you just did.

When I say that the gym isn't a safe place, I mean existentially. It should be a challenging place where people lay their current selves on the line so that they may grow to meet their better selves. And there's nothing "safe" about that process—or, at the very least, safe-feeling about that process. Anything, be it a set of deadlifts or a stiff deadline at work, that serves as a bridge between a current self and a future self has an element of danger. Let's consider that from the perspective of a person budding up against a change via training—it could be you, it could be one of your clients.

First, the thing, whatever it is, must be overcome. That's, well, hard—or it at least it should be. Who knows if you can actually do it? Then there's that whole new identity waiting for you on the other side of the challenge. You don't know that person yet—you don't know how to be them. The current you, you know that person—and he or she is pretty damn comfortable. To be that new person, you'll have to see yourself differently, and, even though that's one of the reasons you're at the gym, it doesn't make it any easier to approach the introduction.

Training presents all kinds of existential dangers that lurk in the shadows beneath each barbell. It accumulates with each added plate. While it should mostly be physically safe, and it needs an environment that promotes psychological safety, it is not a safe place.

Since clients are entering the gym to face an ever-evolving, existentially dangerous challenge, we have to create environments, interpersonal and physical, that promote psychological safety. A single word encapsulates it all: *stability*. If the environment isn't stable enough, it's likely people won't seek the challenges that they truly need—those ones that introduce them to their better selves. There are just too many other "threats" to deal with, and the exploratory parts of their personalities can't manifest themselves. The search gets delayed because there seems to be real and present danger right in front of them. Most of that "danger" is not feeling comfortable with the interpersonal environment. And when the comfort rug is pulled out from beneath our feet, we conserve rather than explore.

## Conservation vs. Exploration

The brain, and the body's, main goal is to stay alive—that means not doing things that unnecessarily expose the body to threat. It also means adapting so that your psyche and biology can manage the environment. We are driven to live, damn it! That means finding a balance between doing and not doing.

Conservation takes place when we don't have a strategy for acting in an environment—or we feel overwhelmed by the amount of variables that we can't account for. There just aren't enough answers to our questions—whether those questions are conscious or lurking below our awareness. And since there are all of these extraneous things to account for, the exploratory parts of our personalities, the parts that seek challenge above and beyond, remain stifled. Remember the conversation about the introverts and extroverts we had earlier? When you can't account for what happens at the party, you end up in the corner staring at Andy Dick rather than taking the risk and talking to new people...that is if you're the anxious introverted type. In the gym, if there's no sense of psychological safety, a person can't embark on the challenging journeys of iron hoisted and lungs burnt that end in transformation.

Without some semblance of social and emotional comfort, as well as comfort with the physical environment, in the gym, folks will conserve. They won't explore, testing their abilities and stretching themselves into change promoting physical and existential discomfort. So, we have to take all of the potential threats off of the table. Now, we aren't able to account for everything, especially at the individual level.     But we have to remove all of the instability and anxiety provoking issues that we can. Then, once we have a stable environment established, both interpersonally and physically, we can help people find a reason to get uncomfortable and explore. Then we can help them excavate their reasons for avoiding conservation and bring them to the surface.

Let's examine a practical, every day example: a client is apprehensive about a certain exercise because they are scared that performing it will injure them. It's a situation that every trainer encounters. Many times, a trainer faces this dilemma even at the beginning of their career. The two predominant drivers of this client apprehension are past injury and unfamiliarity. People that have been hurt before will often psychologically, and physically, guard themselves from any situation that they perceive as threatening. Especially if that situation approximates the one that got them injured. Folks that are new to sometimes training lack the confidence-promoting competence needed to approach an exercise boldly. And it's common that they've heard horror stories about other people getting hurt.

Each of these situations motivates the client to conserve because they don't feel safe in the environment. Under these circumstances, our job is simple: put the person in a position in which they believe they can explore. We accomplish this with two potential strategies—or a combination of each. The environment is changed, shrunk, to make it less threatening. Using the current example, that means changing the exercise, or the variation of the exercise, to one that the client can approach. Or we bolster the client's confidence by giving them a strategy they believe in and can use to approach the exercise that they find troublesome.

The ultimate goal is resiliency—for it to take more threat to affect a person. That means that they are more willing to take on challenges and that they have more strategies for moving themselves forward. The stability of our environment helps them deal with and overcome the instability of other environments. It also means that it takes more physical load to affect their bodies—that's threat, too, ladies and gents. So, as we adapt and grow stronger, our bodies, and our brains, can handle more.

# Psychological Safety: The Two Environments

As we examine psychological safety in the modern fitness gymnasium, there are two main environments that we have to consider—the interpersonal environment and the physical environment. They must be harmonious, each reflecting the other in the gym. But examining them individually will help us blend them in understanding and action.

## The Interpersonal Environment

Individual relationships and the broader social climate of the gym make up the interpersonal environment. Because, you know, all of that takes place between people. And, being people, it's innately important to us to figure out where we fit and how we relate to the other people sharing a space with us. A few of the questions that might roll through our brains, consciously and subconsciously: *Is there anyone here I should be afraid of? What about someone I'd like to see naked? Are there any protectors in this piece? Do I generally have a place here? Am I safe, can I let my guard down?*

Our goal as coaches should be for someone in our space to answer the last question with an unequivocal yes. And we do that by, first, being aware of how important it is—and second by creating a structure, based on that understanding, that allows people to relax. In turn, it gives us the ability to understand the people that want to trust us with their fitness journey. There are three tools that I, and the coaches on our staff at the gym, use every day to stay aware and create a healthy, productive interpersonal environment: practicing unconditional positive regard, utilizing our three personality archetypes, and keeping our own personalities consistent in the gym.

*Tools for Gym Interpersonal Stability*

1. *Unconditional Positive Regard*
2. *The Three Personality Archetypes*
3. *Your Consistent Personality*

**Unconditional Positive Regard (UPR)**

Carl Rogers, the humanistic psychologist that created the term and a guy that we all owe a lot to, believed that people had the internal resources to be self-determined and to develop fully as a human being.

That's the underlying foundation of why unconditional positive regard works. People are people, we have our bad and our good, but we all have the ability to choose our path and change.

Unconditional positive regard is recognizing a person as a human being because you're a human being and you get it—you know what it's like to have quirks and be a little weird, and, all the while, you see your own potential for self-improvement and change. It allows you to recognize that other people have that potential, too—quirk and all. Besides, doing weird things, that even sometimes seem to obstruct our forward movement, is part of being human. It's accepting that. It's noticing behaviors without ascribing a positive or negative valence, without jumping to a final, concrete judgment about a person. This all blends into a neat little unconditional package, one that you present to a person, showing them that they don't need to do anything to earn your esteem.

There is, however, a misconception that UPR is just being nice to everyone all the time, and that's not it. It doesn't necessarily scale beyond close, interpersonal relationships. At times, like in a public situation in which we have to evaluate someone's motives, our regard must be conditional. It's not just a "everything is sunshine and roses" approach to life. UPR has a goal. That goal is growth through honest communication.

Through practicing UPR, we communicate competency and autonomy. The relationship communicates to the people in it that, "You're accepted, you can handle this, and navigate it in your own way. I'm here for support and I'm not going to remove my care for you because you make a mistake." And, "You are worthy of the truth." When a relationship, and an environment, communicates that to a person, watch out, because that person has the foundational goods to skyrocket their trajectory.

The question is, how do we put this into practice?

Watch that first rep and let it suck. There's nothing in the fitness coaching setting that better communicates that "you don't have to earn my regard" more than avoiding immediately jumping in with a correction as soon as a client does something imperfectly. When people get to try and miss the mark without interruption, it subtly communicates to them that they are able to keep trying and that you're going to regard them positively no matter how many times they try and fail. Further, it makes trying and failing safe. If someone were to get smacked with a rebuking correction every time they teetered on the line of doing something incorrectly, they'd stop taking the risks that they need to take to grow. The caveat to all of this, of course, is actual physical safety. If someone is going to do something that will likely injure them, of course you need to stop them. Use your reason to make the distinction between the situations.

Also, remain unflappable in the face of people's weirdness. Weirdness, in this case, is a blanket term I'm using to describe all of the things that people tell us that could be potentially shocking, the stranger parts of people's personalities that they show us, or the crazy shit that clients try in the name of furthering fitness and body composition. When I say unflappable, I don't mean be an emotionless robot. I do mean maintaining a warm, yet consistent demeanor. Let's use an example to illustrate.

Let's say a client shows up for a session and they make some kind of crazy confession. They say, oh, I don't know, that they ate forty-two donuts between four and five in the morning and then, in a sugar-induced psychosis, they French kissed their doorman and took a Fed Ex truck for a three-block joy ride that ended in her actually safely delivering a few packages to the nice people of her neighborhood. Since she did such a good job delivering the packages, Fed Ex decided not to press charges.

Now, there's the human element in all of this that calls us to be enthralled by a wild story—and so we should be. But, see, the client was super-worried that you'd jump on her about the forty-two donuts. She mentions them waiting for your negative reaction, thinking that you'll lay some serious disapproval on her. But you don't. You say something like, "Dang, that's a wild story! Well, do you feel like you're ready to train with what we had planned today, or do you think we need to redirect course?" Then she relaxes a bit—maybe (everyone is different, but most people respond pretty well to not being judged.) She brings up the donuts again, and you say something like, "You keep bringing up the donuts, do you want to talk more about those?" What follows next is a client-driven, client-centered conversation, with a warm, consistent coach, about the donuts and some strategies about how she can avoid this situation in the future, rather than a reprimand from someone who is essentially a peer trying to help them achieve some goals. And, ultimately, options are laid out for her to choose which one might work for her rather than firm directions handed down from her coach. That's remaining unflappable.

Another aspect of bringing UPR into the real world and out of the realm of nice ideas is practicing detached compassion—which is productive, but folks confuse it with empathy. Over the past few years, empathy has buzzed around the fitness industry as the blanket term of choice. But I think that word has walked us into a real Princess Bride situation—*you keep using that word, I do not think it means what you think it means.* I should know, I've definitely mistakenly used it. Empathy literally means feeling what the other person is feeling at the same time. Sure, there are elements of compassion and caring built into the definition, but empathy can't be practiced without concurrently feeling what the other person is feeling. In a coach-client relationship, that's an issue. Coaches must retain some objectivity, some level of detachment, depending on the context, for them to be able to help a person.

For example, a client comes in despondent and despairing over their current body composition situation, and they confide in you these feelings and then explain further that they stem from his overly judgmental relationship with his father. You connect with him empathetically, feeling his despondency and despair, and connecting with him also on the botched parental relationship—you've had a similar experience. Now, you're both caught in a swirl of unrelenting emotions and there's no one left to guide either of you out of the situation. Even worse, there's a strong likelihood that you'll retract your focus from the client and instead focus on your own feelings. When we feel bad, we tend to have a hard time not focusing on ourselves. This, ladies and gents, is not the correct outcome.

Detached compassion, however, offers us the opportunity to notice, and care, without getting caught up in our own feelings. (There's a time for us to be concerned with our own feelings, when we are with a client and trying to help them is not one of those times.) Detachment, in this context, means that we can stay firmly rooted in ourselves and give objectivity a fighting chance. Compassion is the caring element—and in this case, without pity. It's the effort to understand, the person's situation, and perhaps connect some of your personal experience, while helping them improve it without having to feel exactly as the other person feels.

It all sounds well and good, but how do we actually do it? How do we act on detached compassion and keep it from drifting off to the land of forgotten nice words? Awareness is a good start. If you know that you'll be working with a demanding client, or you know you have a propensity to be empathetic, prep yourself by giving yourself some boundaries before you work with, or chat with, someone.

On the other side of empathy is the tendency to be overly judgmental—we're human, judgment's squinty eyes find us all at some point. There are appropriate times to judge, and inappropriate. Working with a client is one of those inappropriate times—judgment, in that setting, spoils unconditional positive regard. And our clients deserve that regard, so how do we combat passing judgement? Curiosity is my favorite weapon.

"I wonder why?" is my favorite question when someone does something, well, human and weird or what would seem counterproductive to anything that promotes progress. Asking, "I wonder why" gets us to think about circumstances and to evaluate a situation dynamically rather than making a static judgment about a person. That simple question gets us thinking about what factors could possibly contribute to a person making a decision. And when we think that way, we can see the person as a person that's moving through the world as a person, doing silly person things as a person often does—rather than some...well, I'm sure there are plenty of unnecessary words that fit there. People are people—and curiosity helps us see them as such.

Now you're armed with a working definition of UPR and ways to practice it—a foundational and actionable coaching philosophy. Let's continue on to the three client archetypes we use to form a basic understanding of client personalities. UPR keeps the relationship open so we can develop understanding and the archetypes help us turn understanding into communication.

**The Three Personality Archetypes: What, Why, and How**

Clients give us clues, some obvious and some opaque, as to how they'd like to be interacted with. Sometimes it's the questions they ask and the statements they make. Sometimes we're only given implications and information to induce or deduce. Using years' worth of observations and interactions, I created three, outrageously over-generalized client personality types. But they happen to be extremely useful when gauging how to interact with a person at a given time. Especially when that time is at the beginning of the coach-client relationship.

The last thing we want to do is put a person in a bucket and leave them there, people are dynamic and respond differently to different contexts, environments, etc. But simple, general tools that create frames and divisions help us to understand and interact with each individual. Feeling heard and understood is something that all people want, and it that feeling goes a long way toward promoting psychological safety.

Our three personality archetypes are What people, Why people, and How people. *What* people just want to know what they have to do to achieve their results, and they put their heads down and go without needing much else from their coach or coaches. *Why* people want sound reasoning and explanations for what they are doing before they totally buy in and expend effort. *How* people are mostly relationship-based. They want to know how you feel about them and how they fit in first, then they can worry about all of the other things.

There's one, gigantic, uber-important thing to keep in mind—we're all, all of these people. However, we each have a predominant modus operandi depending on environment, circumstances, etc. In context, we're talking about how a person manifests their personality with a gym-based, coach-client relationship. It's especially observable, and important to note, in the beginning of the relationship. As time goes on and relationships evolve, people show different parts of themselves. You'll likely see people change archetypes before your eyes. And, mostly, people are a combination of two archetypes. With all that said, there's a predominant one that is usually noticeable from the get-go.

Understand, also, that these three archetypes are just starting points for learning how a client likes to get information, what information is most important to them, and how they want to be communicated with. People are incredibly complex, things will change—but the cool thing is, you'll likely see elements of one of the other archetypes pop up as your relationship with the person evolves, so you'll still have an understanding and a strategy for interacting.

Each of the three archetypes has its own highest value that it's seeking, as well as dangers and pitfalls to avoid. Let's unpack those for each archetype, along with some strategies for combating the dangers.

**What People**

At Beyond Strength Performance NOVA, we have this client named Ron (not his real name, duh.) Ron's laser focused on losing fat while maintaining his strength. The fella is a hulking type of dude. He's also one of the happiest people I've ever met in my life. I've never seen him walk past a person without uttering a hello or a kind word. That was a total aside, but I wanted you to know that about Ron, because, well, it's good to know that there are people like him.

Ron's clear and declarative with his goals. They're unwavering and he takes consistent action towards them. As he states, and acts towards his goals, he gives us his implicit trust. When he trains, he doesn't question why a given exercise, or set-rep scheme, is being used, he just does it with the faith that we've made the best possible decisions we could make to put him in the best possible position to be successful. When we meet about his programs and his goals, his half of the conversation is seasoned with deferential statements. Most commonly, "I just trust you guys to do the best thing for me."

Ron is the perfect illustration of a classic What person—he gives implicit trust, his highest value in communication is the result, he's devoutly committed to his goals—acting consistently to progress toward them. He just wants to know what he has to do, and he'll do it.

For example, before he started training with us he was following a ketogenic diet but stopped as he joined our gym. Problem was, he was in the habit of eating super high amounts of fat, and he continued to do that even as he started eating higher amounts of protein and carbs again. So, as he began training with us he was getting super-strong, super-fast, but he was gaining weight—something he didn't want. Knowing something was up, he scheduled a consultation with our nutrition coach. As they laid out his current diet, it was glaringly apparent that the fat intake was the weight gain issue. It was recommended that he alter his fat intake back to normal levels, and he did—without question. Then he started consistently losing weight.

The highest communication value for the What person is clear direction toward the result. Yes, everyone wants results, but for What people it's that simple. With the other archetypes things get a little more convoluted and other questions need to be answered before results become the primary concern in communication. What people are simpler. As long as they are seeing progress, they are typically happy. Keep them moving forward at consistent increments and your relationship is typically in good shape.

What people seem like a dream, right? What danger lurks in the recesses below their outwardly trusting cooperation?

The danger begins with the 'if a little is good, more must be better' mentality. It's a commonly, but not necessarily, manifested complexity of the What person archetype. Their sincere, but misguided logic follows: *they like to work, and they just want to know what to do, so if they do that thing they are supposed to do, maybe they should just more of that thing they are supposed to do, and they'll get to their results faster.* Every trainer has at least one client like this throughout their career. The client that takes the good they're given and overworks it. How do we combat this and help the client?

One early step is asking for their trust in the process and laying out clear steps that they can follow—inside and outside of the gym. If they want a detailed "what", give that to them. Work with them to gain clear direction for what they should be doing on off-days, how to follow their programming using the right amount of effort in the gym, and fill in all of those other little gaps that they could fill with unnecessary amounts of a good thing. A full plan and buy in goes a long way to help the over-working What person, but sometimes a dose of "whoops I shouldn't have done that" works well to curb their excesses. Pause and take a breath before you read the next paragraph.

This is going to seem outwardly counterintuitive, but I promise I've seen it work for the chronic 'more is better' sect of What people. Let them mess up. That's right—let them overwork a bit, let them go to excess and try the crazy diet, let them do too much on their off-days. Some What people just have this need-to-abuse-a-good thing wired into them, and they need the experience of burning themselves to the ground to break the hard wiring. But here's the deal, a coach has to be there to support them and provide context after that mess up—using tools like rating of perceived exertion to give them info about appropriate effort. Sometimes people have to go to a dark place to learn where the light is, and it's not because they aren't willing to listen to you. They just need to find out. That's one of the downsides that I've noticed about some What people. Even though they just want to know what to do, they also want to take that What and make it their drug. Sometimes it's appropriate to give them the room to do that.

We're also in danger of letting a What person's outward front lull us to sleep. It's easy to assume everything is all good all the time, limiting our check-ins and efforts at relationship building. You know the old adage *the squeaky wheel gets the grease?* Well, What people predominantly aren't all that squeaky, so while other people are more demanding of our time and attention, What people get passed over and the depth of the relationship with these folks gets ignored. While the relationship may not be as outwardly important as it is to a How person, it's still important—they are human beings.

Overcoming this danger is simple, don't ignore the relationship. As obvious as this may sound, learn about the person—seriously. Outwardly it will seem like the depth of relationship doesn't matter as much to a What person. But taking the time to ask questions and learn about what else is important to them will go a long way toward retaining that client, which ultimately helps them to achieve what they set out to do. Change is the product of consistent effort, and it's impossible for an unretained client to be consistent with you. Beyond that, we can't disregard the human element. Human connection is one of those three big reasons people come to see us, that doesn't change just because it isn't a What person's highest value. It's still a value.

Another danger is the Faux-What person. This subtype is a people pleaser in disguise as a What person. These folks outwardly appear as What people because they just want you to tell them what to do. The big difference, however, is that they're seeking that direction because they want your approval. While there may be an implicit trust, it's convoluted by their excessive need for you to think favorably of them. Before we go any further, I think it's important to note that I'm not making any kind of diagnosis here—I'm not a psychologist or psychiatrist. I'm just giving you information based on years of coaching, research, and a solid, fundamental understanding of psychology—as psychology is understood up to this point in human existence.

I'm not certain why these people-pleasing, What people behave as they do, but, from what I've observed these folks lack the direction of a classic What person—and they're looking for someone to give it to them. They don't want to commit to their own goals or lack the security to set their own. Their refrain goes something like this, "Oh, you just tell me what I should do." The very real danger here is these folks will completely introject what they think your goals for them should be without taking any steps to project their own vision and clear their own path. Accompanying that danger is the likelihood that they'll become too dependent on seeking, and receiving, your praise—turning your coach-client relationship conditional instead of an unconditional. No bueno.

WHAT's a coach to do to avoid this? (See WHAT I did there? Ok, I'll stop.) While this is a complex situation, as most human situations are, there are two simple things that a coach can do to combat the over-dependence of the Faux-What person. This list, mind you, is not exhaustive, but it gets the party started.

First, when you notice that they are behaving like a What person without the serious, secure direction of a classic What person, pay attention to that. In a lot of cases, they'll start down the path of asking you what their goals should be. When this happens, set the boundary that you can't be the one to set their goals for them. This sounds like a sticky situation if you have no real way to guide people through a goal setting process, but you have to stand firm in that. We'll also be getting into goal setting later in the book, so you'll have some tools if you are currently sans a goal setting practice.

We, as coaches, can't waffle on that boundary. If we do, we make things worse—our jobs get harder and we make things less secure for the client. So, when they lean on you to tell them what to do or what their goals should be, lean back a little and say something like,

"I'd love to walk you through a process of setting goals that mean something to you, but I can't be the one to give you those goals. Would you like to talk through some goal setting?" Keep in mind that how you make this statement depends on your relationship with the person. It should keep the spirit of the statement above, but it doesn't necessarily have to be so stiff and clinical.

If they don't want to have that conversation, that's fine. It's totally ok if they continue to train without a super-precise direction—often times the act of training helps a person develop a direction that they didn't previously have. Action always helps. But, here comes a broken record—we can't give them a goal or series of goals. Goals are something people must set for themselves, especially in a close client-coach relationship, because if they just take on the coach's goals and values the relationship becomes convoluted. That convolution inhibits the client's ability to progress, as a person and in the gym, and de-stabilizes the interpersonal environment.

The second thing you can do in this list o' two strategies is create opportunities for the person to praise themselves rather than you praising them. It sounds awkward, but it seriously works. Rather than saying something like, "Good set, Janice!" after your client, who is, of course, named Janice, completes a successful set, ask her what she liked about the set.

This gives Janice the opportunity to self-praise, but also reinforce her knowledge of the movement she just completed. That, ladies and gents, is a what we call a double whammy.

Here's a bonus strategy to add to the list—creating a culture of peer reinforcement. And, when I say peer, I mean client to client. For those of us that work mostly in the small group personal training and group setting, it's easy to pull this off. It really starts by fostering relationships between clients and helping them get to know each other. The easiest way to do that is to fill the space between your walls with quality people and lead from the front by showing people, well, that you actually give a shit—a big one. Then do stuff outside the gym to help people interact in a different context and get to know each other as people. It works—like, really well.

As you create that culture, people will often just automatically jump in to support each other. It creates a self-sustaining, positive environment that you foster but don't have to actively prod and push. The environment becomes its own, autonomous, positivity and growth-promoting animal. There's a distinct beauty in it. People help people and grow closer to one another, and all you have to do is start it with a little nudge then sit back and watch as you fine tune and keep things on course.

To take things up a notch, we've also added a Personal Record Bell to our gym. Here's the rule—only clients can ring it for other clients. And, in reality, there doesn't have to be a PR for the bell to get rung—it could be for anything one client wants to recognize another client for. It's pretty cool.

Wrapping up the chat on the Faux-What person, keep a few things in mind. I'm not recommending becoming some unfeeling robot that only creates distance. What I am recommending is awareness and boundaries. They'll help everyone.

And, to close the conversation on What people in general, keep a few things in mind. Help them turn their clear direction in to simple, definitive actions. Remember to develop the relationship even though the result is likely their highest value. And, when necessary, give them the room to mess up with a little bit of overworking, but be there to give context and guidance so they can learn from their mistakes.

**Why People**

In the past, I had the opportunity to work with a baseball pitcher that had the fortune, and misfortune, of being 6'3" when he was twelve years old. Being twelve years old, and someone that grew like a rocket was strapped to his back, he didn't have the strength, resiliency, control, or sustainable capacity to handle the stress of pitching. The outcome? An elbow injury and Tommy John surgery at the age of thirteen. Super.

What happens when a smart, cerebral thirteen-year-old kid is sidelined with injury that doesn't allow him to do the thing he loves the most, and, in the process of training and rehabbing, you don't give him any answers, or value the fact that he's interested in and needs some answers? Something that looks like outward de-motivation and low-effort.

This kid, we'll call him Gerald, had seen physical therapists and trainers after his surgery for a couple of years before I met him and started working with him. He came across as morose and disinterested, but as I got to know him, I realized he was a bright, curious kid. He'd also just spent two years rehabbing and training for a sport and still hadn't played. At some point, anyone would start asking what's all this for? Why am I doing all of these things if I'm not even getting to do what I want to do? Gerald hadn't been given any good answers.

My boss at the time noticed that I'd developed a good relationship with Gerald, and when it came time to write Gerald's next training program, my boss asked me if I wanted to take over his training. It was a smart move on my boss's part. Not because I'm some programming wizard, but because he understood the power of connection and what it does to help people make progress. I, of course, agreed to take over. Gerald and I got to work.

Knowing that Gerald was a cerebral kid that liked to know things, as well as directly connect his actions to his goals while understanding the reasoning, I asked him if he wanted me to explain his program and why I'd made the decisions that I did. And when he acknowledged that he'd like that, I laid it all out for him, explaining why I had made every choice and how each of those choices related to where he currently was in his training process, as well as how it connected to getting him back on the field.

I continued to explain things to Gerald and encouraged him to ask questions. It was as if he became a different kid—at least in the walls of our gym. He was seeing progress and he understood why. An adult was also treating him as though he wasn't just some kid that needs to "just do what he's told." (Quick aside: I'm not saying that any of the other coaches at the gym I was working at were just telling Gerald to do the work and keep his mouth shut. That's not the case at all. What I am saying is that my developing a relationship with Gerald and understanding of his curiosity helped me to better help him.) Then I took that to the rest of the coaches. But sometimes when the answers someone wants aren't given to them, and they're not acknowledged in the way that they'd like to be, it's implied that their need to know doesn't matter—even if that's not the intention of the coach.

Gerald needed to know why. He needed to be able to connect his actions with sound reasoning, and when he could do that, there was a different sense of motivation. The morose, "lazy" kid morphed into a funny action taker—it was a beautiful transformation to watch. (He went on to play college baseball, by the way.)

Our man Gerald is a classic Why person. The Why person's highest value is knowing. It's most important to them to make the connection between their actions—the actions their coach is recommending—and their desired outcome(s). These folks aren't just innately curious, they also don't like to act without justification. When they don't get that justification, their effort is either entirely stymied, or, at the very least, lacking strongly concerted drive. If their need to know why isn't met, and they aren't acknowledged for the intelligent human beings that they perceive themselves as, they won't buy in. (Fun fact: I'm a Why person through and through.)

The biggest danger associated with Why people is treating them as if they are What people—expecting their trust while giving them direction without explanation. It's not that Why people are natural born a-holes that just like to push buttons or ignore a coach's advice. Needing to understand is just part of their motivational make up, and it's how they like to be communicated with. Combatting this danger is simple—have sound reasoning for everything that goes into a Why person's training process. (P.S. You should have sound reasoning for everyone's training process, it just has to be super-tight with Why people...and well-communicated.)

Why people are going to ask...well...*why* something is in their program, so an arbitrary exercise selection that you haven't totally thought through is an absolute no-go. Because if you do make such a choice, and you hesitate when they inquire, that hesitation won't go unnoticed. And then you'll lose some relationship footing with that lady or gent. But, if you reason through all of your exercise, and coaching, selections for that person, and can explain how every piece relates directly to their goal-achieving process, then you're in solid shape.

That includes avoiding exercises that you're not totally well-versed on—even if you think it might be beneficial for the person. Let's say you just got back from a great, weekend seminar and you learned some intriguing exercises that you can't wait to put into practice, but you aren't totally comfortable with the cueing, where the exercise fits in someone's program, and clean performance. Don't experiment with that exercise using an inquisitive, Why person's program. Your lack of true understanding will be noticeable and will definitely impact rapport. If, however, a person likes experimentation, and you have a conversation with them beforehand that lets them know you'll be playing around a bit, then you're likely ok. Not outwardly acknowledging the experimentation it is the issue.

In most instances, if an exercise, a set and rep scheme, an exercise sequence, a change in process, is happening and it involves a Why person's process, have a true and confident understanding of the change and explain clearly why you're making, or recommending, the change.

Get comfortable saying, "I don't know, but..." It's a phrase that serves us all well in many parts of our lives—keeping us open to possibilities and demonstrating that we are intelligent enough to realize how little we can be sure of. And, in the case of building a relationship with a Why person, it builds trust with them. Why folks have extra sensitive bullshit meters, so if you lay some on them thick, they'll sense it and the entire game will be afoot! Saying, "I don't know, but..." and either finishing that sentence with, "I think..." or "I'll get you an answer" will absolutely build trust between you and a Why person. You'll, of course, have to make good on your promise to get an answer.

Keep in mind that Why people also like to supply answers and demonstrate what they know. These folks value intelligence, and they like to be asked questions as much or more as they like to ask them. I promise you that they know a lot about at least one thing—ask them about it. And, in many instances, they'll value an opportunity to show you that they have training knowledge as well. Give them that opportunity to show you.

Let's level on one last Why person danger—they can wear on patience. Their natural inquisitiveness can sometimes seem annoying, especially if we aren't in the right head space. I'm sitting here, as the coach writing this book, telling you that Why people have gotten on my nerves before and I didn't do a good enough job working with them because of it. I tell you this because, well, there's no high horse for any of us to be perched on. We're all going to mess this up sometimes. But I'm also telling you this to help prevent you from walking into that trap—or at least limit the damage.

If you know that you have a Why person coming in for a session or meeting, especially an expressly inquisitive one, make sure you're in the right head space before you meet them. Have something to eat so that you can better regulate your emotions. Remember, also, that you're their coach and it's your job to answer their questions and guide them into the best possible position to be successful. Physiological self-care and a small bit of framing goes a long way toward keeping your relationship with a Why person on the up and up. Seriously, at some point this is going to matter.

To wrap up the Why people discussion, keep in mind that the "why" is what these folks need to buy in to your coaching, programming, process, what have you. Offer them sound reasoning and only use exercises and methods you're well-versed in. Don't forget to ask them a few questions, and, for the love of everything holy, don't try to bullshit them.

**How People**

Once upon a time a coach named Wendall worked for us at Beyond Strength Performance NOVA. Wendall definitely wasn't his real name, but he did really work with me to coach our afternoon training sessions. Everyone loved Wendall. No matter what was going on in his life, he showed up to work with a smile on his face, and, with his crazy antics and obvious, deep care for everyone he worked with, he put a smile on everyone else's. Wendall was never afraid to express who he was, and that made it easier for everyone around him to do the same.

I opened up the shop every afternoon, and I'd be there for at least an hour before Wendall rolled in—he was our evening closer, staying until the last clients finished up around 8 p.m. During the beginning of our tenure together, I noticed something peculiar. If we were busy when Wendall walked in, or I was focused intently on something, and I didn't make a fuss over his arrival, he was a little withdrawn. I'll follow that statement by saying most of the time, and especially when I noticed my attention affected him, I greeted Wendall loudly with jokes and hugs. But I noticed how much my lack of affection affected him, so I made sure that every time Wendall walked through the door, he received all of my attention—if only for a moment.

Wendall's highest value is the relationship and knowing that he's accepted—I know, it seems counterintuitive based on his ability to show himself in all his grandeur. But as it goes with most things, context is king. Sometimes it's simply a reinforcement of relationship from someone they value. Being that the relationship is his highest good, he's a How person. He wants human connection first, then he can get to the part where he does his best job.

How people got their name by the implied, and sometimes not so implied, question that their behavior asks—*how do you feel about me?* In many instances, they are also folks that consistently ask how to do something—even when it seems like they should have that something down. Maybe it's an exercise, or how
to read their program, etc. I can't give you a definitive reason why, but I've noticed a connection between these two types of "hows" over the years. And they've combined to construct the general How person archetype.

These folks tend to question their competence more than they should, and they outsource it to coaches in a different way than a What or Why person might. Sometimes it happens as a social phenomenon, other times it pertains to skills, and still other times as both. That want for competence, and potential feeling of lack, is something that we must consider even more intently than we would for one of the other client archetypes. We have to put them in positions for success early and often—especially in the realm where they feel the most incompetent. To do that, we do as much as we can to match the interaction, and the environment, to the person's current level.

Let's say, for example, that a person new to your gym that's introverted and has mentioned that they also don't like to be the center of attention. Also, this lady or gent, happens to feel particularly nervous about learning how to deadlift—they've been fed a lot of foolish propaganda about how deadlifts are dangerous body destroyers that turn your back into a pile of mush and give you kidney stones...or something like that. They aren't totally convinced of that nonsense, they think if they do deadlifts correctly they'll be fine. But, none-the-less, this person still feels some apprehension and is painfully aware of their lack of skill. So, the absolute best thing to do is just load some weight on the bar, walk them over to it, and make them get over their fear while also crowding around other clients to observe. I'm kidding, please, for the love of Christopher Walken, don't do that.

It's imperative that we set this person up with a situation that allows them to jump over a "small hurdle" first so that they feel success as early as possible. To do that, we have to consider their "hows" in each realm—social and exercise performance—and put them in the position that doesn't overwhelm them. Let's have a look at each individually.

Maybe your protocol is to introduce a new member to as many people as possible on their first day. It's always good to get people together, right? And maybe that introduction is a public one that consists of you yelling across the gym, "Hey, everyone! This is Charlene! She's new and we're pumped to have her. Everyone, say hi!" Which, in most respects is awesome—and it just might make Charlene, that introvert that's concerned with not being the center of attention, come out of her shell. But, from the evidence that she's given us, it probably isn't the best move on day one. She likely needs some warm-up time. It would probably be better to explain to her the normal protocol and see if she's comfortable with that, and, if she isn't, do something she is comfortable with. A few quiet handshakes and hellos with your most welcoming members is probably the best move. Unless she says she'd rather keep to herself. In that case, do that. The best policy is to ask.

Once you move past the social realm, and onto getting Charlene picking stuff up off of the floor, it's time to consider the best place to introduce your new friend to the wonders and splendor of loaded hip hinging. By this point hopefully you've completed some kind of movement screen that gives you the low-down on Charlene's movement competencies and capacities. This will be your secret weapon for starting her off in the best possible position to be successful and get an early win.

At my gym, we use the FMS with some accompanying tests as our movement screen. So, I'm going to speak from that point of view to paint you a picture. To keep things simple, let's say Charlene is a 2/2 on the active straight leg raise and she can touch her toes—meaning she has all of the proposed movement capacities required to full range of motion deadlifts. Knowing, however, that she has no skill and experience with deadlifting, and that she's apprehensive, I'd start at the lower end of my deadlifting progression—at a level where she'll likely learn quickly and experience immediate success. Then, using another small increase in hip hinging difficulty, we'd progress to increase skill. When we found the hip hinge variation that challenged her enough to continually build strength and skill, without putting her in a bad position, we'd stop there...and that would be the movement that stuck for her first program.

(Quick aside: I'm describing a process we use in our personal orientation sessions. Each client in our small group personal training program gets an individual session to learn the main movements at our gym and for us to learn what movements are right for their first program with us.)

Charlene, the fictional person that she is, just experienced our process that we call small hurdle, big hurdle. It's a simple way to introduce exercises, challenges, etc., that match clients' current level of perceived competency and willingness to seek challenge. The goal is to increase the size of the hurdle the person is willing to attempt to "jump." Every person needs a combination of small hurdles and big hurdles, the proportions of each are individually, and situationally, dependent.

When it comes to How people, a series of small hurdles to get the party started, get momentum rolling, and get some competency-laden confidence building is usually a great initial course of action. Sometimes it takes a series of small wins to show people how capable they truly are, and how quickly they can become competent at something that scared the living bejesus out of them. Once there's momentum, that's when bigger and bigger hurdles can be introduced. Helping them celebrate the success of jumping over those small hurdles helps to accelerate the process. We have to draw attention to the fact that they just did something good and celebrate that with them. Celebrate even the smallest of victories. It helps the rapport of the relationship, it ensures that they aren't skipping over their accomplishments, and it builds their confidence in their competency.

Having objective markers helps How people navigate the world of hurdles and challenges. Overcoming something, no matter how seemingly small, gives them the opportunity to prove their skill, strength, and growth to themselves. Sure, everyone on the planet benefits from the process of overcoming something difficult and seeing themselves grow into someone more capable. How people are just more sensitive to the effects. At our gym, we have strength standards that folks must pass/demonstrate proficiency with before they're allowed to move on to barbell work, overhead training, and push-ups from the floor. Since we've been talking deadlifts and Charlene, let's keep it consistent and stick with those examples.

In the back corner of our group training floor there sits a 60-kilogram kettlebell—that's 132 American pounds. A lady or gent must perform two, consecutive sets of eight reps with good form before they can move on to any kind of barbell deadlifting. (The next step in the process is the barbell RDL.) Charlene is interested in deadlifting, even though she finds it a little intimidating, and wants to be able to, not only move on to bigger and better deadlifts, but also prove to herself that she's strong enough to handle it.

By the end of her second program, she nails it and is absolutely elated. I'm seriously sitting here as I write this trying to think of a better way for someone to prove to themselves that they're capable, and I can't call one up. The small hurdles introduced to Charlene on day one of her training helped her build the momentum that empowered her to jump over the big hurdle of passing the deadlift standard. That's small hurdle, big hurdle in action. (P.S. This isn't just some cockamamy story that I made up for illustration's sake. This happens at our gym consistently—every day, every week, every month.)

So far during our How people discussion, we've talked tools for putting these folks in the best positions to be successful—but what about the dangers associated with How people and navigating those?

Remember our discussion on the Faux-What person and how their approval seeking can transform your unconditional relationship into a conditional one? The same danger exists for How people. Since we are their coaches, we are often perceived as being in a, de-facto, "one-up" position, rather than just being their peers. Since How people are focused first on relationship, acceptance, and appearing competent, it's easy for them to get locked into the habit of seeking a coach's approval. We nip this in the bud the same way we do for the Faux-What person—get to asking them questions so that they can reinforce themselves as soon as possible and create an environment of peer reinforcement.

Another, much simpler danger, is mistakenly treating a How person as if they were a What or a Why person. It's a simple case of mistaken, or disordered, values. Of course, the How person still wants the results, and there's probably some part of them that's curious about the process. But it's not their initial highest good. Beginning from a place of What or Why puts the relationship too far to the side. That's another no bueno situation.

Keep in mind that these dangers aren't certainties. I'm not saying that every How person will absolutely try to shift the relationship to a dependent one by seeking your praise, it's just something to be aware of. I mention this because these folks still need your praise and demonstration of acceptance—all that celebrating small victories stuff we talked about before. We just need awareness of dangers, and strategies, so that we can navigate those dangers should they show themselves. So, don't withhold praise from someone that needs it just because you're worried about them becoming too attached to you. And trust me, you'll see the warning signs if they are heading that way. No matter the case, it's always good to create an environment where people can self-praise and garner strength from their community of peers.

In closing, How people value relationship and feeling competent above all else. That's their entry way into communication and learning with you. Show them immediately that they are unconditionally accepted, give them small hurdles to jump and build confidence in their competency, and celebrate the hell out of those successful hurdle jumps. Create an environment in which they can self-praise and garner strength and support from their fellow members. Do all this, you'll nail your How people relationships.

## Determining Archetypes

All of this info on the archetypes is great, but it opens the door for a seriously big question: *just how in the great blue blazes do you figure out which archetype category a person falls into?* Fair enough. Let's get you an answer.

In the words of my mentor, Bill Hartman, everything is an assessment. The process of determining archetypes begins with simply paying attention and listening to what the person is saying to you. And when I say listening, I don't just mean noting that they said they want to lose body fat. I mean hearing them say that they want to lose body fat, getting curious about why they want that, and then asking questions that allow them to expand...then continuing that process to infinity and beyond. It's the curious mindset that's absolutely necessary. That's what we need to actually listen.

A framework for questions is a big help at the onset of a relationship when the focus is getting beyond the surface and truly getting to know someone. In the book *The 7 Levels of Communication*, Michael J. Maher introduces the acronym FROG to ensure that we are asking questions that help us get to know people in the areas of their lives that are totally relevant to them. It stands for Family, Recreation, Occupation, Goals. Asking questions in those areas, while putting on your curious mindset helmet and paying attention, will give you a great deal of information about what archetype category a person mostly fits into. Run their answers through the filter of the highest value that each archetype holds dear and you will gain some clarity.

We also include a question on our intake form that works wonders—*how would your best friend describe you?* Yes, that totally sounds like a cheesy, dating site profile question, but if you think about what a question like that actually accomplishes, it doesn't seem so cheesy.

That question gets people to describe themselves without actually making them talk directly about themselves. Having to think directly about yourself, and then state that answer—especially to someone that's essentially a stranger—is tough for a lot of people. But if we can move just the slightest bit adjacently, and get them to think about how someone close to them would describe them, they describe themselves by how they think they are viewed. Which, fundamentally, gets them to describe themselves. That description will give you a great deal of information about what archetype category, or categories, someone fits into. Again, run that answer through the filter of the archetypes and their highest value and you'll have a great starting point.

Now, that we have all of that out, let's talk about a few things to keep in mind with these archetypes.

First, keep an open mind and don't get locked in on what you suppose is the perfect archetype for a person. There is no perfect. These are starting points that allow us to apply trial and error during our interactions so that we can learn about, and understand, someone. If you practice this process a lot, you'll get good at it, and you'll make better initial assessments/guesses/whatever you want to call them. But, remember, these are just starting points that give us an idea about what is important to a person and the information that they most want to interact on first. These aren't simple classifications of human beings. That would not be fair. As you interact more and more with a person, you'll learn more and more about what is specifically important to a person...because, well, if you do the whole relationship dance well, they'll tell you. These archetypes just get us moving in a good direction.

Second, this isn't a science. Sure, these archetypes are the outcome of empirical observation over the duration of a coaching career, but this isn't some area of research you can look to for confirmation. It's based on my scientific, and human, understanding of people and applying that over and over again in different environments and contexts. But I don't have any specific research to necessarily back all this up.

Third, it's rare that people fit into just one archetype category—they're often two. I just created the three archetypes to keep things simple and make delineations that make it easy to observe, note, and act. As your relationship with a person evolves, they'll reveal different parts of themselves and you'll see the dynamic combination of their values in action. And it's totally likely that their highest value will shift as their relationship with you, and your training environment, develops. Constant curiosity and constant vigilance will help you note it and maintain the relationship accordingly.

Fourth, each archetype spans the traditional personality spectrum. There are How people that are extroverted and What people that are introverted—vice versa. Some Why people are laid back and Type B, others are hard driving Type A pushers. As much as it would make life easier, none of the archetypes, at least that I've noticed up to this point, fit neatly into personality definitions. That's because most people don't fit neatly into any definition. Each individual is the outcome of millions of years of evolution, life experiences, current environment, inherent proclivities, etc. So, while we use simple archetypes to help us to begin to understand someone, we cannot neatly connect them to other specific aspects of personality.

These archetypes are simple tools to help us learn about people and interact with them in a way that is important to them. That's it and that's all. We can't become robots with this stuff and just jam people into metaphorical boxes and keep them there. Being a real human being and developing real relationships is always the coach's highest good. At the risk of sounding like a broken record, I'll repeat again—these client archetypes are just a starting point for helping us learn about what's important to a person and interact with them accordingly.

Beyond being mindful of the person in front of us and working to understand them, it's equally as important to be mindful of personalities and how we are bringing ourselves to the coach-client relationship. A bit of self-understanding, and consistency in self-presentation goes a long way.

**Your Personality**

When I was in college, I was a student supervisor of the Lycoming College Recreation center. I absolutely loved it. For a few shifts per week, I'd hang out in my office adjacent to the weight-room, which I thought was outrageously cool, check on the other students that were manning other parts of the recreation center, get some school work done, socialize, and make sure everything was locked up at 11 PM when the center closed. It was my college, meat-stick dream job—and to make the deal even sweeter, I had an incredible boss. She's still my favorite after all these years.

Her name was Laura, and everyone called her LJ—combining her first and last initials to create her nickname. She was the perfect person to supervise people in their late teens and early twenties. LJ was warm, welcoming, encouraging, and also a strong source of accountability. There weren't any fast ones pulled on her, even though some tried. I never wanted to try to get away with any shenanigans while I worked for her. I cared about her way too much, and I knew truly how much she cared about me.

That was the thing about LJ—she made us want to be a part of something, and work hard—together. She didn't just give us a list of job tasks and hold meetings to make sure that everyone was on the same page to get the work done. She created opportunities for us to grow as people as she consistently helped us develop personally. Consistency, for all of the other endearing words I can use to describe LJ, is her best descriptor. Her presentation of self was always consistent, and she consistently did her best to make us better.

In her efforts to make us better, she'd have us report early before the fall semester to do some team building and workshopping. Some of us, being athletes, already had to be on campus. But the others showed up, too—another testament to LJ. During those few days, we'd get to know each other better, do some writing about what we want and where we want to go, and have some fun...all while planning out how the next semester of work would be carried out. One year she introduced us to the FISH! Philosophy—the customer service culture building resource from the people at the Pike's Place Fish Market, a place wildly popular for how they make customers feel about their experience while perusing fish to buy or just showing up to watch folks sling fish back and forth.

As a staff, we watched a video that presented the FISH! Philosophy. I remember one distinct part about choosing to be where you are when you're there. One of the fish mongers was talking to the camera, and he mentioned that he was out late the night before. He'd only slept for a couple of hours. But he still showed up with a solid attitude and worked hard. More than a decade has lapsed between when I saw that video segment and the time that I'm writing this, and what that guy said still sticks in my brain. He wasn't a miserable sumbitch because he was tired and *had* to be at work. He chose to stay out the night before. He chose to be at work. He chose to have a good attitude and bring his best to the job.

These lessons stuck with me when it came time for me to begin directing internship programs and developing staffs of coaches. We must have a consistent personality. And we must remember that the work we do, and how we approach it, is always a choice.

## Expectations Must Match Experience (Or At Least Get Damn Close)

I travel to teach...a lot. And, thanks to the development of the internet and the app-reinforced mobile phone, I spend a lot of time being carted between airports, hotels, and gyms by Uber Drivers. There's always an air of the unknown when ordering an Uber. Who knows if the person picking you up has people locked in their basement and likes to collect kidneys? It's exactly the opposite of what our parents taught us growing up—never get into a car with a stranger. But, for the most part, the situation plays out the same way. A seemingly decent person that's just trying to make a living picks you up and takes you safely to wherever it is you'd like to go...even if they make a couple of wrong turns or get lost for a minute or two.

During one such traveling teaching gig, I landed at the San Francisco International Airport and called for a ride to San Mateo, a town not far away. When I first connected with the Uber driver, he called me, and seemed pleasant with a welcoming tone of voice. His questions and comments made me believe that he was generally concerned about my welfare and providing me with expedient, safe travel to my hotel. My expectation was to meet a pleasant man and have some polite conversation on the ride to the hotel. That didn't happen.

When I stepped into the backseat of the car I fired off a polite, genuinely excited, "Hey! How ya doin'?" not even trying to hide the Central Pennsylvania, podunk accent and nearly embarrassing niceness with which people where I'm from treat strangers. His only reply was, "Are you Todd?" and he didn't even turn his head examine my face. Both hands remained on the wheel as he stared straight through the windshield. I acknowledged that I was, indeed, Todd. A head nod let me know that he heard me. That was it.

As we drove off, I took one more stab at making conversation. A lot of folks tell me I'm weird, that they'd rather not talk to Uber drivers—they actively, and sincerely, hope for a silent ride. But I can't help it, I like to talk to Uber drivers and learn their stories. People, to me, are supremely interesting. I wanted to know what brought this man to the Bay Area and led him to use his time driving strangers to and fro. Besides, I think acknowledging another human in a shared space, and showing genuine care and interest, is a beautiful thing that we should all do for each other. I'm aware that not everyone shares my philosophical sentiments.

My attempt at conversation was met with, what seemed to me at the time, sociopathic silence. How did this man, so genial and welcoming on the phone, morph into the silent assassin that was clearly driving me to my death? "Great," I thought to myself, "I'm about to become a rusty basement science experiment. Well, good luck with my hemorrhoids, fella!" Of course, my brain was just going to a ridiculous place. I made it safely to my hotel. But the experience wasn't pleasant. Sure, maybe I'm a little crazy, but I think most folks in that situation would be at least somewhat off put by the discrepancy between our phone conversation and our in-person meeting. The unmatched expectations provoked anxiety.

Consider this in your coaching context. What expectations are you putting out into the world with your forward-facing image? Are they being met daily when clients interact with you? If not, congruency must become a priority.

## Inconsistency Breeds Insecurity

We inherently want to understand our environments and we want them to be stable. Welcome back to the discussion on conservation vs exploration. Stability, consistency, and predictability allow us to relax. When our perception of any of those things is skewed, our threat meters send up a flag and tell us to conserve—to protect ourselves in some way, however small. Inconsistency breeds insecurity. That's especially true when it comes to how we present our personalities

every day at work and with the relationships we build with
our clients. If people aren't sure what version of you they'll meet every day when they walk into the gym, they're going to be apprehensive—then the protective mechanisms of the ego get involved.

Let's posit that one day you're super positive, outgoing and a general joy to be around. But during the following three days you're withdrawn, quiet, and irritable. We'll go on to say that this is the general cycle in which you show up to work with your clients—maybe the ratio of days changes slightly. Your clients can never be sure which person they're going to meet when they show up to train. The only expectation that they can truly bank on is the uncertainty of the interaction—you might be a dream, or you might be withdrawn and morose. This is, of course, an extreme example, but interpersonal inconsistency, even when it's happening at a lesser degree, will likely cause people to self-protect in some way. What I've noticed during my career, both when I've had my own personal ups and downs in the past and as I've witnessed from other coach-client relationships, is that folks will behave in one of two ways: they'll withdraw, keeping some kind of distance (even if at the surface agreeable) or they'll try to please you to meet the same end.

Neither of those scenarios are productive for the client—and they aren't any good for you either. Both interrupts a client's ability to trust you, train, and get results. And, there's a good chance, they each end in the client leaving you to find another solution. At the very least, creating an inconsistent interpersonal environment by not maintaining a consistent personality when working with your clients causes relationships to suffer. Life is a relationship business, and our livelihood is an exponential magnification of it. Without the ability to build and maintain relationships based on consistent, sturdy footing, we are dead in the water.

Here's the real deal—I'm not on some high-horse preaching at you. Every human has ups and downs, some have a lot more downs than ups, and vice versa. (General outlook on the world, however, seems to play a role in the percentage of each that person encounters.) Keeping ourselves consistently acting the same way at work isn't always easy, and there are going to be times that we absolutely fail. That's why we need strategies to do our best at keeping those failures at bay and fix them quickly when they do happen. We're human, too. There are times when our clients should see other parts of us, more of the full story. But it's not during the time designated for them—the time that they are paying you to help them grow. It's their time, and that must be held sacred.

Reality is that there's a healthy range that we all must live in. We're not always going to be at our most outgoing or our most reserved. But there's a consistent range, and consistent qualities, that we can demonstrate so that we maintain a stable interpersonal environment. What's most important is keeping away from the absolutes and the extremes so that our clients can predict, consciously or subconsciously, what to expect from us day to day.

At our gym, all the coaches have noticeably different personalities, some more outgoing and, well, a little off the wall, while others are a bit more reserved. We all, however, bring a committed consistency to our jobs. There are a few different strategies we use to keep ourselves level and consistently bringing the same self to the job every day. Let's examine them, working from the biggest rocks down to the smallest ones.

## A Coaching Code of Values and Success Checklist

Consistent action isn't just something that we can pull out of our asses every day. We need guides and reminders, based on what we believe would be the ideal conditions, to help us shape our behavior throughout our work and our lives. These guides and reminders must be written down, constantly visible, and referenced as often as possible. We use two such guides at our gym—our Coaching Code of Values and our Coach's Success Checklist. The Code of Values is the philosophical foundation of ideals. It is a list of ideas that encompass our over-arching philosophy—*human development for development's sake*. We attempt to act on our philosophy every day, between the time when we first open the doors in the morning until they close each evening. The ideas expressed in the code expand on human development for development's sake and what it takes to live that philosophy out.

Our Coach's Success Checklist is the guiding rubric for daily action in our roles as coaches. Where the Code of Values is a source of inspiration, and an expression
of ideals to be constantly strived for, the Coach's Success Checklist directly defines daily actions that help us perform our jobs to the best of our ability—and in a way that carries out the ideals expressed in the Code of Values. Also, and maybe more importantly, the Checklist defines success for us all. It says, "Do these things and you will have nailed your shift."

There's one more, pivotal, thing that the Checklist brings to the table—a process for consistent self-evaluation and improvement. It asks each coach to review the items on the list at the end of each shift, evaluate themselves on how well they carried out each item, make a rating, and then make a plan to improve their performance in their weakest area during their subsequent shift. So, not only do we have a rubric that exactly defines what success is, we also have a way to evaluate where we were most and least successful, and then make a plan to improve.

These two tools, employed in tandem, not only create a growth-centered environment based on high ideals that are constantly sought after and embodied, but also give us a means to bring a consistent self to our jobs every day. They provide the simple boxes that need checked to ensure that we are showing up in the same way all the time.

Here's the biggest point to be made about the Code of Values and the Success Checklist—they aren't just nice ideas thrown up on the wall. There are lots of businesses that publicly post their core values and mission statements, and they're absolutely full of shit. They're just pleasant words that live in the sugar-coated world of gilded pleasantries and people willing to lie about them. While the Code of Values and Success Checklist are posted on a wall in our gym for everyone to see, we didn't just hang them up there in some silly effort at virtue signaling. We check in on them consistently at team and individual meetings, and we truly hold each other accountable to living them out in the real world. That, friends, goes a long damn way toward promoting consistency.

## The Table of Stable Growth

Showing up consistently as a person your clients can count on is easier when your life is in balance—or at least when you have an awareness and understanding when you're out of balance, and what you could potentially do to rectify it. Without balance, or an awareness of our imbalances, it's difficult to be level because our perception of the world is being assaulted by threats that exist just beyond the extent of our knowledge of them. We can't be sure what's wrong or what to do about it, so we often end up riding an emotional roller coaster that carries us along a track of inconsistent behavior.

It isn't easy to gain that kind of insight without an illuminating tool, some sort of metaphor that allows us to think critically about our lives, evaluate without unnecessarily harsh judgement, and plot a plan of action. We need something that helps us categorize aspects of our lives and separate them for examination, prioritization, and action. Enter the Table of Stable Growth.

Throughout my life and career, I've spent a lot of time studying great organizations—from businesses to sports teams. Those that I've admired most, like the New Zealand All Blacks, have some sort of tool that they use to stay balanced, set goals, and improve as people. As I set out to create a unified team at Beyond Strength Performance NOVA, I thought to myself, "Well, shit Todd, we need something like that." I don't always talk to myself in the third person, but when I do it's usually out loud and in some place where in which people can immediately notice and judge me as a dangerous, crazy person.

Rather than just adopt one of the tools/metaphors that the folks I admired created, I decided to create one specific for us, one that applies to our lives as coaches. Sure, it can be more broadly applied, but my thought process started with the things that are most difficult, but also most necessary, for fitness industry coaches to keep in balance. Well, actually, it started with a wobbly table.

I was sitting at a coffee shop, getting judged by hipsters for not wearing the appropriate flannel, attempting to work and sip on some coffee. But every time I moved, not only did I get a shifty glance and eye roll from the super hip, forearm tattooed, beard oiled, Brad-Pitt-haircut-from-the-movie-*Fury*-having gentleman behind the counter, but my little cafe table also wobbled all over the damn place, nearly spilling my coffee every time. This was, of course, at the time when I was trying to construct our metaphorical tool for life balance. And bam! It slapped my right in my balding head. Life as a table with four legs that must be held in balance.

I thought back to the four big areas that started to suffer in my life when I got busy as a coach, and that also outrageously improved my life when I started paying attention to them again: *professional development, personal development, physical development, and enrichment (which breaks down into fun and/or spirituality)*. The bolts that fasten the legs to the table are actions. They are the things we do that keep our attention locked in on developing in each area—to keep each leg stable. Things like reading and attending workshops for professional development, training ourselves to keep on top of our physical development, and just doing a few things we enjoy, to ensure we are still having fun. If we are consistently acting, we are consistently tightening the bolts that keep the legs fastened securely to the table—avoiding the unbalanced wobble. Trouble is, it's not always easy to keep tightening those bolts.

When we first get busy as trainers and coaches, it's common for the physical development leg to be the first one with loosened bolts and wobbly posture. The Greek myth of Tantalus becomes apparent in real life. Tantalus was condemned to an eternity standing in a lake under a fruit tree. Every time he'd bend over to take a drink, the water would recede, keeping him from every quenching his thirst. The fruit tree was equally as torturous, eluding his grasp every time he'd reach to pluck something ripe from its branches. Our place of employment becomes Tantalus' lake and fruit tree. Every day we are surrounded by equipment and people training—we even train people to improve themselves, but we can't "find" the time to train ourselves. Even worse, we lose the commitment and motivation to even want to train ourselves. As this persists, our physical instability worsens.

This process of progressive destabilization happens with every leg of the table—sometimes all at once, other times in series. And, since the table is a simple metaphor for life, as the table destabilizes so go our lives. Consequently, its damn hard to bring the same, focused self to work every day when the different parts of your life have gone awry, or if one leg of the table is outrageously wobbly—especially if you're lacking awareness of it.

Having balance, or at least having a distinct understanding of why we are unbalanced, helps us manage the affective tumult of life. Balance means that we don't have to slip back into conservation and live defensively. We're free to be open, explore, and share the best parts of our personalities and selves. If total balance isn't possible, which it often isn't, then having the Table of Stable Growth to use as an awareness tool gives us the opportunity to notice what's up and then make a plan to rectify the situation. That clarity, that knowing, that ability to realize that the current state isn't permanent, and having a strategy to do something about it, gives us the ability to steady ourselves. Steadiness is absolutely key if we are to be the person that our clients need us to be day in and day out.

Examine your current life as it relates to a stable table. If it's sturdy as can be, great! Pay attention to what you're doing and keep going—with the knowledge in the back of your mind that it probably won't always be this way. Mindfulness is your weapon when a leg gets wobbly and you have to shove some sugar packets under that sucker. If you know you're wobbly right now, look at the areas that need the most attention, make a plan to start there, start small, and act. You can balance your table, make it sturdy, and place all of the good things that you want in life on top of it. That realization will help you be an even better coach to your clients.

## Leave Your Shit At The Door

Before each of his shifts at BSP NOVA, Wendall, the coach we talked about during our discussion on Why people, sat in his car for five minutes. He wasn't mindlessly scrolling through Facebook or checking the latest sports scores—he was meditating. Each day before his shift, he took five minutes in his car to breathe, empty his mind, and create a barrier between the rest of his life and his work. Wendall consistently coached his ass off and brought his best self to the job every day, and during his time at BSP NOVA, he always had a lot going on in his personal life. I'm not saying that it was just that five-minute, daily meditation that gave him the ability to compartmentalize and coach, but it was sure an integral part of the process.

That was Wendall's strategy for leaving his shit at the door so that he could walk into the gym ready to be the best part of our clients' day. It's one of the rules we all follow. Whatever we have going on in our lives, we do whatever we have to do to leave it at the door when we come in to coach. For us, it's a conscious process. Sure, it seems obvious, something we should just "know" to do. But, here's the thing about those things that we should just know to do—they often don't get done unless we're paying attention. So, we pay attention.

We all have our own processes, whether it's just making sure our table is balanced or meditating in the parking lot, to make sure that we are ready to go every day that we walk through the door. No one is perfect, we're not going to be at our full capacity all of the time. But what we can do is get the absolute best out of the capacity that we do have for that given day. The funny thing is, as we commit to a process that helps us check our shit at the door, we need it less and less and our capacity increases.

Whether it's taking a few minutes to breathe, making sure you get your workouts in, or doing something else to create a buffer between the potential negatives in your world and your coaching shift, figure out what you need to do to leave your shit at the door every day.

### What's My Purpose Right Now?

A few years ago, I read the book *Improv Wisdom* by Patricia Ryan Madson. This great little book is full of insights from the improv and theatre world that help improve our communication, connection, and, well, just life in general. It's definitely worth the short amount of time that it takes to read.

One of her tips, for life in general, is to ask ourselves what our current purpose is. The human brain is a crazy place for a person to live, and it's easily lead astray by a million and one internal and external stimuli concurrently romancing and bedeviling it. There are always the crazy thoughts like, "I wonder what my dog is thinking right now?" or "Isn't it crazy that the human brain actually named itself?" Don't spend too much time on that last one, it'll take you down a doozy of a rabbit hole. And there are also the outward perceptions of our environment and the current conditions that we have to process. There's always a lot of information coursing between our synapses. We, at times, need simple tricks for snapping ourselves back in.

Let's say you've had an exceptionally busy day of coaching. You've already completed eight, one-on-one sessions and you have three more to go before you're done. As you start that ninth session the fatigue covers you in an oppressive cloud of self-pity. You start to notice how tired you are. You start to wish you were somewhere else. Gasp! You start to hope that your last couple of clients for the day cancel so you can just go home, put on Spongebob and eat Fruity Pebbles in your Superman pajamas. (P.S. We've all been there with that feeling of self-pity and wishing the day was over. If we hadn't there'd be no need for this section of the book.) If you continue along with that line of thinking, there's a great chance that your last few sessions of the day are going to be absolute poop. That whole consistent personality thing that we've been discussing dissolves into a cloud of "I don't give a shit anymore, I just don't want to be uncomfortable." But your clients deserve better. Hell, you deserve better from yourself. These destructive feelings must, and can, be defeated.

When that sorry-for-yourself storm forms on the horizons of your mind and starts setting in, interject with the question *what's my purpose right now?* It's the Northern wind that clears the self-created storm from your mind and saves you from yourself.

We'll continue this discussion by holding the premise that you deeply care about your work and you have a strong, personal reason for why you do it. That "why" that everyone talks about these days—a foundation necessary to weather the storms of self-pity and lack of focus that will inevitably hit. A foundational purpose
is the personal GPS that helps redirect course and choose a purpose of the moment when we are losing direction and focus. If we know, and maintain a consistent vigilance, that our foundational purpose is human development for development's sake, we can

distill that down into a current purposeful thought and action that coincides.

We'll continue with the example of that ninth one-on-one client the cloud of self-pity. You know, however, that your reason for training is to help people to develop, to grow to become more, because it's imperative for their quality of life—because you know what it's done for your quality of life. Embodying that philosophy, one that you remind yourself of daily, you say to yourself, "Ok, sexy, what's my purpose right now? Is it to be home and comfortable or is it to give Mrs. Jones a great session that helps her move forward? Obviously, it's to train the shit out of Mrs. Jones. Snap back in, and let's do it."

Knowing your overarching purpose, and then having a way to snap yourself back in during those periodic lapses of forgetting it, will bolster your resiliency and keep you consistent.

## The Interpersonal Environment in Closing

There's no denying that the X's and O's of training are fun. Picking the right exercise intervention for a person at a given time and understanding the dynamic interplay of programming, adaptation, and physiology is super cool, if not super nerdy. But still cool. There's also no denying, however, that we're in the people business. No amount of X's and O's knowledge is going to get the job done if people don't feel connected to the person, or people, supplying that knowledge. We must create an interpersonal environment that not only connects people, to us and to each other, but that also supply the preconditions for self-challenge and self-growth.

We do that by understanding people through frameworks like What, Why, and How that illuminate for us what different people value and how they want to be interacted with because of those values. Presenting ourselves in the same consistent, positive way at work every day is also one of those things that we do. Don't expect yourself to be a super hero, we need checks and balances, tools, that give us the means to examine ourselves and act so that we can bring our best selves to our coaching—day in and day out. If we focus on those two things, and commit to nailing them, our interpersonal environment is maintained, and remains, a steady supply of support and energy.

Let's move from the abstract world of the interpersonal environment to the concrete land of the physical environment.

## The Physical Environment

Let's imagine walking through a forest—one totally unfamiliar to you. You don't know the trees or the paths. The animal sounds are strange, you're in a different part of the world—not the park or the woods of your youth. Maybe you walk straight through, machete in hand, confidently bushwhacking your way to discovery with a complete disregard for danger. Some folks are wired that way. Most of us, however, aren't. It's more likely that each of your steps would be cautious, your eyes wide and focused searching for movement among the trees, a displaced leaf or a shaking bush. You'd peer intently around each bend, and hoping that there isn't something, or someone, dangerous on the other side of the next tree. It's human—we move cautiously in unfamiliar, and potentially unnerving, places. The gym, for a lot of people that hire us for training, is one of those places.

Clients new to training, or just new to your gym, are scanning the environment, whether they know it or not, for potentially anxiety provoking threats. They're looking for all of those animal sounds coming from somewhere they can't quite see. We call them the metaphorical "tigers in the bushes." Our job, as coaches, is to kill as many of those tigers as possible so that our clients can relax, and take on real challenges, much sooner. There's no way to account for all the potential tigers that may exist in the mind of a client, and we also shouldn't totally try to morph the environment to accommodate one person, but there are general tigers to be slain that make the physical environment much more mappable.

As a client continues on with you, and evolves from someone new to someone constant, they have a better handle on the environment. They have it mapped. But that doesn't mean that the tigers aren't still there, they are just latent, resting in the bushes and waiting for us to stop looking. We can't stop looking. Maintaining a consistent physical environment, controlling all of the factors that we can control, helps a client to explore rather than to conserve. There are three things, when done consistently, that keep the physical environment approachable for your new clients and your vets.

## Maintaining the Environment: Ordered, Understandable, Ritual-based

*Where do I go? Who will be there to meet me? What does the place look like? What actually happens?*

These are the questions either consciously, or subconsciously, going through a new, or potential, client's mind as they set on coming to train with you for the first time. There are tigers hidden all through those questions—and we kill them with three, sturdy weapons: order, an understandable flow, and a consistent/ritual-based process. Those weapons not only lessen a new member's anxiety and show them that they are welcome and wanted, but they are also the tools of consistency used to maintain a stable environment for veteran clients. All of them are inseparably linked in real-time function, but for the sake of discussion we'll dissect them.

**Order in the Gym**

There's a running joke at Beyond Strength Performance NOVA that Chris is the Order Nazi. Each plate has its place. Like things must stay neatly together. And those damn kettlebell handles better not be askew at the end of your shift! Actually, it's not really a joke—that's how we do things at our gym. Everything has its place and each thing must neatly find its way back to its assigned place after each use. At the end of each shift, things get straightened to as close to perfection as humanly possible.

You might be thinking, "Keep things clean and tidy. Ok, cool. Got it. Why in the hell are we talking about this?" Fair question. Well, because the order of the external environment in the gym is reflective of everything
else. Disorder tells a story—one about incompetence, disorganization, and anxiety provoking threats at every level of a person's interaction with you, your training, your business, what have you. It also creates

disorder in the mind—there's a reason that our parents harped on us for keeping our rooms clean when we were kids... they weren't just being tyrannical overlords giving us meaningless tasks for the pleasure of watching us suffer. They knew that disorder in one part of our lives creates disorder in the others. When a person walks into an organized space there's a better chance that their brain can function in an organized way. The uncertainties seem limited, making it much easier to map. No matter how long a client's tenure with you, this will remain important.

Let's illustrate a few things that we do to maintain order in the gym. We'll start with the gym in a broader sense and then consider more specific actions—like setting up for a one-on-one session.

This is going to sound a little insane but nearly everything in our gym is symmetrical. The same amount of plates is stacked on each weight tree. Like plates go together. Kettlebell handles are set parallel to each other, etc. Symmetry communicates order and it saves the brain a lot of energy in trying to figure out patterns. Humans like to see patterns. Creating a mostly symmetrical space helps clients to see those patterns.

The idea comes from Gestalt psychology. Well, the idea is much older, but the understanding we have of patterns and how we perceive our world was championed by German folks at the Berlin School of

Experimental Psychology. Their main thesis was that the cognitive process creates a whole from its perceptions that over-arches the constituent parts. Kurt Koffka, a leader of the Gestalt psychology movement,
is famously quoted as saying, "The whole is something else than the sum of its parts." And we apply that whole, that pattern, from our perceptual fields into our understanding. It's why we immediately see a face when we look at the front of someone's head, and we have to focus to segment out the constituent parts—the nose, mouth, and eyes. We see the pattern first.

A symmetrically ordered gym makes it easy to see the pattern, rather than having to search and search to make sense of the constituent parts and construct a whole image. Thinking in a broader sense, we want clients to construct a positive whole as they think about our gym. The symmetry and order of the gym is one of the constituent parts, and if it is off, and doesn't match the other aspects of their interactions with your gym, your process, or your training, then they can't possibly construct a totally unified whole. That's incredibly unsatisfying to their brains, and it also creates a level of inconsistency that lets tigers lurk in the background.

I'm not saying that you have to be a crazy person about this, but symmetry, balance, and order do a lot to help people make sense of your space. Think about how you can organize your space(s) so that they have some semblance of balance. Commercial gym trainers, you're probably like, "This sounds nice, but I don't have control over a lot of this." Don't worry, I got you with some answers that are coming in just a bit. Hold tight.

Ok, symmetry, and the explanation behind why it's important, is cool and all, but what about other, simpler things to do to keep the gym in order? Well, remember that "everything has its place" statement from the beginning of this section? At least do that—and not like kind of. Before becoming a gym owner, and seeing the absolute importance of having order in the gym, I worked at other places that *kind of* had a place for everything—but everything was still kind of a mess. And it was reflected in all of the other processes in how we ran things at the gym. Reserving a designated physical place for each thing the gym, and making it look nice when it's in that place sends, the message that your proverbial shit is together—the little things always impact the big things. And when clients see that, it reflects back to them order, and their brains can relax.

Beyond maintaining symmetry and having places for things—clean. Clean all the time. At BSP NOVA, we re-order and clean things at the end of every shift. Now, we aren't talking a full scrub down, but all of the bench surfaces are wiped, handles on the suspension trainers are also wiped, dumbbells and kettlebells are ordered, and all of the other things find their way back to their respective places. It gives the coaches closing the shift a ritual wind down to end their work, and it ensures that the space is put together for the next time clients roll through the door. Clients deserve the opportunity to enter an ordered gym—if that's totally controllable for you. If it's not, in the case of a commercial gym trainer, you have to control what you can control to create order.

While you can't order the entire gym as a commercial gym trainer—the chaos of gym members, other trainers and all of the other wild shit that takes place during commercial gym life, puts a damper on your control—you can create a little corner of order for each client. Here's a suggestion: get as much of the equipment that you need for the session contained to a small space, have it set up in the sequence it will be used, make sure it's set up orderly, and clean it before the client uses it. That's a little island of orderly sense in a sea of chaos.

Cleanliness and organization may not be the sexiest coaching book topic that you've ever read about, but it will seriously improve your clients' perception of your space and help them save a lot of mental energy. Focusing on the little things will also help you function better as an individual, and, if you run a team, it will help the unit function better as well.

### An Understandable Flow

A client should never be confused about what comes first and what happens next. The flow—from your overall training process to the day-to-day movement through the gym—should be easily communicable and understood. If it isn't, everyone, including you as the coach, has to spend time and energy every day figuring out just what the hell is going on. That's not good. Remember, inconsistency breeds insecurity. And a lack of understandable flow in your training process and day-to-day training lays the insecurity down like a thick coat of French fry grease just waiting to send someone head over heels and onto the hind parts.

Speaking of French fry grease, think about how things work at any fast food franchise. A person walks in and they immediately are directed to where they should walk to form a line. Then they follow the line to order. After that they receive a sack or tray full of MSG coated deliciousness and go on their merry way to indigestion and fart-coated burps. But the flow of the place is immediately understandable and actionable. (Also, get off your high horse, you know you've had fast food before.)

We can learn a ton from franchises, because they have to make things so simple and understandable that they are replicable a million times over by a hundred-million-thousand people. The employees have simple tasks to understand and follow, and those that patronize the establishment don't have to do a lot of thinking about how to move through the space. Their energy is spent on ogling the menu for super-caloric mouth fun. In our setting, the training, the programming, the community, and the coaching combined are the "super-caloric mouth fun." We need to make the movement through our process and space easy and understandable so that fun is had by all.

It begins with communicating as much as possible about how your training and coaching process works before a person ever even steps foot in the gym—this goes for gym owners, commercial trainers, and independent trainers alike. At BSP NOVA, when someone signs up for a consultation, they receive an email with absolutely everything they need to know to understand what will happen during the first consultation and how that will affect their training. During the consultation, the flow and process are explained in more detail. They get the entire deal up front so there are no surprises. Also, the process is simple. It's not some convoluted, hyper-complex load of shit that makes us look cool. We make the process of getting started at our gym, and following the training process, as simple as possible. It goes:

> *Consultation—>Orientation—>Get program—>Train until program is complete—>Meet about program—>New program—>Train until program is complete*

That process continues on for as long as someone is our client. There are two different types of meetings held during this process, and we'll cover them a little later on. But the flow is simple, and it's communicated early and often.

Our day-to-day gym flow is equally as simple—and it's also communicated early and often. We'll talk more about how it goes down in the next section, but the important thing to keep in mind during our current discussion is that it makes sense. Certain types of training take place in certain areas of the gym—and those certain places allow clients to move through the gym sequentially in an understandable flow that leads them from start to finish, from warm-up to cool-down. It's as if each training session is familiar, but enjoyable, journey. Clients go to a designated place to begin their journey with a warm-up and power training, which leads them to the next place where they work toward climbing a peak with their strength training and conditioning. After that, they come back down the other side to gather themselves with a cool-down before they move on with the rest of their day. And all of that takes place in a flow that leads them into and out of the gym in a way that makes common, easily-understood sense.

Even for you folks that don't have total control over your environments, commercial gym trainers and independent trainers, I'm looking at you, it's possible to create an understandable flow for your people. Create that little corner of order that we talked about earlier. And organize that little corner of order in a way that the client can move through it sequentially, and progressively, with a simple, understandable flow. Meet them at the same place every time. Guide them to a place where everything is set up for them to take a familiar journey.

I am, however, under no illusions—I know you commercial and independent folks won't be able to manage this perfectly every time. But if you manage it as well as possible, and pick a few things that you can consistently nail to create a flow for your clients, your life will get easier and they'll be able to focus more on the work they are doing rather than figuring out just what is going on.

The brain's energy economy is cheap—it wants to save wherever it can. Familiar flows help the brain save energy so that it's there to expend in focus and effort in ways more productive to individual growth. Consistent rituals nested within flows help even more.

### *A Consistent, Ritual-Based Process*

Every day when a small group personal training client enters our gym they know that their program, clipped to a clipboard along with a pen, will be waiting for them on the window sill just to the right of the main door. If the clipboard is laying down, they know that there isn't anything special to pay attention to. But if it's standing up, it's a reminder to notify a coach about something—an FMS re-screen, or it's the last day on their program, or they are reaching the end of a block of programming. Every day, their program is there waiting for them—provided that they did their part and scheduled.

Once they find their program, they write in the date of their session in the blocks at the top and fill out the daily readiness questionnaire on the back. After that, they take the 100-foot walk down the turf to our warm-up area and begin their training day with, well, a warm-up. Which, by the way, remains constant unless someone has special requirements for an individualized warm-up. Then the person trains with the guidance of their program. When they've finished training, they cool down, return their clipboard to the top of the filing cabinet and place their program in the "daily" folder. Our group training clients follow a similar ritual. It helps us all avoid the unexpected.

Humans, typically, don't like anomalies—they tell us that there is something about our environment that we don't understand. And if we don't understand something, there's a potential threat in that something. So, we'll feel like we need to either figure it out, get away from it, or withdraw inward in some way to protect ourselves. None of those things are productive in a training environment—remember conservation vs exploration. Now, in our environment, it isn't necessarily likely that someone is going to see an inconsistency and necessarily jump right to thinking "stranger danger!" But lack of ritual and consistency has an unsettling effect on the brain because it is much harder to form sets of expectations. If they can't form a set of expectations, then they can't discern what they need to do to successfully act in an environment. That's a problem.

Rituals, like order and an understandable flow, save energy for the brain. The consistency allows someone to understand and act in an environment with a quick handle on things without too much mental effort. If the process is constantly in flux, then people have to sort that out far too frequently. Inconsistency breeds insecurity—it also wastes a ton of mental energy that could be spent focusing on the day's work. But that's not all that they do.

Rituals also serve as a focusing buffer between one segment of a person's day and the rest of their lives. Now, maybe more than ever, people need those buffers—everyone has a ton going on in their lives and things are far more complex than they were even a decade ago. More things vie for our attention. There are just more things to decide not to look at. Processes that happen every day give people an opportunity to shut that out, if only for an hour or so.

A consistent process gives a person a chance to say to themselves, "I do this, now." It's the gateway to a productive session—focus needs a stimulus. Humans, on average, aren't great at just deciding that they'll focus. Sure, some folks have the ability to just flip a switch—and sometimes all of us have that super power. But, even for those folks that seem to readily display that super power, I have a crisp one-hundred-dollar bill that says something environmental served as the trigger, or, at the very least, helped. Consistent daily process, ritual, is that trigger—that helper.

Visualize this:

> *You're a client at BSP NOVA. As you walk through the door, you enter to a chorus of hellos from all of the coaches that are working and some of the clients that are training. You turn to your left and your program is waiting for you. Picking it up, you turn it over on the clipboard and fill out your readiness questionnaire. Then you head down the turf toward the warm-up area and a coach greets you with a high-five and asks you how you're doing and what you want to get done during your training session that day.*

That's the consistent experience our clients have every day at BSP NOVA. It's the ritual. It's the buffer. Without it, it would be much more difficult for them to shut out the rest of the world and just train. Without it, they'd spend time every day trying to figure out exactly what is going on—and they'd waste a ton of energy in the process. Energy, in today's attentional economy, that they don't have to spare if they want to train with focus and also perform well in the other parts of their lives.

Maybe you already have a consistent, ritual-based process like this. If you do, fantastic. Keep it going. But also keep in mind that there is always room for fine tuning. Constant vigilance on our processes is a must for creating a better environment and experience for our clients—and also for ourselves. If you don't have a process like this, it's never too late to start. It doesn't have to be perfect, it just has to exist. Start with one thing, nail it, and make it consistent for your clients. Then, once that's solidified, add in something else—and so on, and so forth.

Commercial gym trainers and independents, this is especially important for you since there are so many other factors about the gym that you can't control. The broken record is about to play again—control absolutely everything that you can control. Whatever it is that you can do to create a consistent ritual, do it. Maybe it's greeting your clients at the same place for every session. It could be having them walk through certain steps at the beginning of each session that helps them create a buffer. It doesn't have to be perfect, it just has to exist. Seriously, get started.

Consistency and ritual are the glue that bind the physical environment. Order and flow start the visual perception that the space is psychologically safe, and the consistent process shows people that their perceptions were correct. We need expectations to make our actions make sense. We need buffers between our training and the outside world. Rituals accomplish both.

## The Physical Environment in Closing

Order, a flow, and ritualistic consistency—creating a physical environment that encompasses all of these elements gives clients a better chance to relax and feel "safe" in your space. By no means am I arguing that people are delicate flowers that must be catered to at all costs. But I am saying that people want to map their environment, have it make sense, and understand how to move through it without a lot of thinking. And giving folks the opportunity to do that by creating a consistently ordered and sensible environment allows them to attach to your coaching much more quickly. People have the resiliency to deal with a lot of environments, but if we take the silly little things off of the table it gives them the opportunity to realize the unsafe part of the gym—the part where they challenge themselves and find out what they are capable of. We can't let the physical environment get in the way of that.

## Psychological Safety in Closing

There are, at all times, two environments that combine to create the overall gym environment—the inter-personal and the physical. When we engineer them in a way that keeps things consistent, limiting anomalies and helping people feel heard and understood, clients have a stable platform from which to launch themselves into a challenge. It's our job to keep them on the path to exploration and avoid slinking back into a conservative withdrawal from what they are capable of.

An interpersonal environment that welcomes human understanding and takes stock of individual personalities, and meeting those personalities where they currently are, helps to drop walls that people would normally erect for self-preservation. The consistency of our own personalities as coaches further keeps those potentially insecurities at bay.

Keeping the gym, or each section of it that you can control, ordered, understandable, and consistently ritualistic saves folks the mental strife of mapping the environment for themselves. People want to feel competent in each environment that they navigate, and if we can make that easy for them, they can expend more energy toward training hard.

Psychological safety is the feeling of acceptance and connection in a consistent environment. It's a precursor, for most training clients, to challenge. When we create it, everyone wins, and we can do a better job guiding our clients through the training process and onward toward their goals. Let's move on to construct our second pillar of fitness coaching—Guidance.

# Pillar II: Guidance

"They keep messing up my defense!" A high school defensive coordinator bellowed to his head coach. I was standing behind them on the sidelines, observing. The year after I graduated college, I coached high school football at my alma mater, coaching the linebackers and helping out with the quarterbacks—the two main positions that I played in high school. The defensive coordinator mentioned in the above quote was someone I coached with, and looked up to, for a long time. But, things had changed.

At the time of that quote, I was a strength coach there to watch some of my athletes compete. I'd often take my Friday nights and cruise the sidelines of Central Pennsylvania football games to support my guys and watch them display all of the hard work they'd done. A few of the kids I trained were busting their guts on the defense that was "being messed up." Philosophically, the defensive coordinator and I had drifted miles apart—continents apart, is probably more accurate.

He kept mentioning *his* defense as if he had birthed it from his hairy loins, as if it were solely *his* possession to ogle and admire. The defensive coordinator's focus was on how the boys were playing with his creation, *his* work of art, *his* baby...*his*...*his*...*his*. At one level, he's correct, he created the defensive scheme by amalgamating ideas from other coaches and acting on years of experience as a Pennsylvania high school football coach. That much is true. But it's the focus on the creation that is telling of purpose and philosophy.

By consistently making statements about how the kids were messing up *his* defense, the coach demonstrated a fatal coaching flaw—he made it about himself and his own glorification. The kids were there to act appropriately in his playing scheme so that he could look good. It was as if he were the savior, the hero, who had given the team his genius in an effort to save them, and they had ungratefully wasted it. That may not be apparent in the words on this page, but it had a profound clarity as I witnessed it and talked with the coach after the game. And I was heartbroken. It wasn't what I knew coaching could, and should, be.

As coaches, we create so that others can succeed—we act for the sake of others. I'm not saying this with an air of martyrdom, though coaching does require some level of sacrifice for others. I am saying that it's not about us. I'm saying that *we are not the hero*. The clients, the athletes, the people that we help—they are the heroes. We are the guides, and we have to remember that. It's a simple shift in mindset. Let's unpack the high school coaching situation described above from the mindset of the coach as the *guide*, and not the savior or hero.

A coach, in the mindset of, and acting as, a guide creates the defensive scheme (or in our case an exercise program or coaching system) so that it puts those carrying it out in the positions to demonstrate their own skills and achieve their own successes—individually and as a unit. The scheme is created for the betterment of the people using it. The scheme is a guiding light that shines on a path, that when followed with enthusiasm and consistency, produces success for those following it. And, as a result, the people following the lighted path end up in a better place. A coach, one with their philosophy grounded in the belief that they are there to support rather than save, to shine a light so that others may act courageously in pursuit of their desires, and a mindset that reflects it, thinks and behaves differently than one focused on themselves and the beauty of their scheme. (Fitness coaches, read: program, coaching system, coaching cues.)

We are not the hero, we are the guide. With that in mind, we approach our work humbly to create so that our clients may benefit. We create for the sake of the people that trust us to help them.

## The Main Goal of Our Guidance

Can you imagine trying to drive somewhere that you've never been without a GPS? If you're currently over 30 years old, you probably remember a time before GPS' when maps were still in their glory and gas station attendants still filled a dutiful role as local expert on whether or not to avoid Walnut Street and take Mulberry. Now, every phone comes with a built in GPS and a robotic lady's voice that offers not so subtle directions. Want to go somewhere new that you aren't sure how to get to? Just drop the address into the GPS app on your phone and it'll spit out the likely best course to get there. If the route gets obstructed or declines in quality, you'll be redirected to a better route.

That's the main goal of our fitness coaching—to be each client's GPS. We help them set the destination that they want to reach, we help them plot a course to achieve it and direct them along the way, and we help them redirect course when they run into obstacles. Our guidance helps people figure out where they are currently at and plot a course toward their desired outcome. And no matter the result of their action, whether they achieve their ultimate outcome or not, they grow through their interactions with us. In practical language, with some influence from the legend Dan John, the goal of our guidance is to *set the goal, keep the goal, and struggle toward the goal.*

It starts with giving them the space, and/or means, to express their goals. Some people know what they want, they see it clearly. Others have a vague idea but aren't totally sure how to express it. Others still, have no idea but they know that they need help because they want to change. Being someone that, at the very least, a client can express a goal to is a huge part of the process. Giving them a structure to set, and monitor, goals is even better. When there's a structure that gives people the means to set goals, continually touch base with them, and see incremental progress, it's much easier to keep the goal. Then, their struggles are validated. We can continue to guide them through those struggles.

Our guidance offers our clients the conscious means to struggle purposefully—a process that's lacking most everywhere else in contemporary life. Things now-a-days, at least for most of the Western world, are pretty damn easy—at least to just stay alive and have base needs met. But there's still this part of our DNA that's expecting things to be hard, and when they aren't there's a void. Unfortunately, that void is usually filled with professional sports fandom, chili-cheese-diarrhea dogs, and a whole lot of wishing things were different. A purposeful struggle, like following a consistent, transformational training process makes people feel alive. There's a body of evidence that says exercise is the best thing to maintain IQ and brain health throughout a lifetime—usually IQ declines with age. I have a theory that's because exercise tells your body you're still alive—that it's still worth maintaining that brain because the person using it is on the move and living.

We are designed, evolved, whatever you want to say, for struggle. Human beings function best when they see
a goal, they expend effort toward that goal, and they see incremental feedback that they are getting closer to their goal. The brain gives folks all kinds of rewards for living out that process—and gives more rewards for seeing incremental progress toward a goal than actually achieving the goal. We are supposed to be on the move toward something life sustaining, whether that's physiological or existential. And our coaching support gives people a means to live out that process.

The main goal of our guidance is to create a process that gives people the opportunity to state a commitment, and take consistent effort toward that commitment, so that they grow. The ultimate outcome—they transform in a way that they desire. There are three big things that fitness coaches must create to successfully guide their clients toward that ultimate outcome.

# The Guidance Big 3: Structure, Accountability, Teaching

Like creating psychological safety with a stable interpersonal environment, coaching guidance has three big components. And, also like psychological safety, really the three pillars of coaching as a whole, the three components of guidance, let's call them mini-pillars, blend seamlessly throughout the coaching process. But, for understanding and improvement's sake, we draw divisions so that we can examine, reflect, and act. Guidance's mini-pillars are *structure, accountability, and teaching*.

## *Structure*

Transformation requires a process. It'd be lovely if one day we could just wake up and say, "Ya know, I think I'll be this now. I'll look like this. I'll act like this. And I'll have a whole lotta zeros stacked up in my bank account." But that's just not how it works, and honestly, as we gathered from our discussion on purposeful struggle, it probably wouldn't be as lovely as we picture it being. We'd be bored, the world would be a bit grayer, and gratitude would be an obscure word hidden somewhere in the recesses of our vocabulary.

Transformation requires a process and engaging in the process can be fruitful for its own sake. There is, however, no fruitful engagement without structure.

Here's the thing about transformation—it doesn't happen by accident. Maybe, hidden somewhere in the annals of history, there are a few cases of people just "waking up different." But it's certainly not the predominant reality. Transformation is a labor-intensive combination of awareness and action. The whole shebang begins with awareness—awareness of where you currently are and the discrepancy between your current place and where you'd like to be. Action is layered on top of that awareness—when we know where we are, and where we'd like to be, we can act accordingly while staying aware and keeping a constant vigil on the outcomes of our actions.

Coaching structure is the scaffolding that, at first, allows people to climb to a better vantage point so that they may view themselves from a different angle and take accurate stock of where they currently are. That same scaffolding then allows them to climb further by giving them the action steps, the rungs to place their hands and feet, so that they may achieve whatever it is they are seeking. Structure is everything that is used to help a person set, and struggle toward, their goals.

It's your programming. It's your cueing. It's your introduction to exercises. It's the goal-setting meetings you have. It's the goal-setting process that you introduce your clients to. Structure is the culmination of everything you do to help your clients—in organized form. *In organized form* is the absolute key phrase. Understanding, and documenting, all of the pieces of what you do so that you may make them consistently replicable from client to client, even if you're a one-person operation, is essential. It's the only way to ensure that your clients receive a consistent product, and it's the only way to surely monitor what you're doing, do more of what's working and disregard what isn't.

We'll talk more about the actionable steps of our structure throughout the rest of these pages—accountability, goal-setting, and all of the other bits of coaching that go into client experience are part of the structure. We'll tackle them individually, creating grand picture of what a coaching structure is.

In the meantime, think about what you currently do with your clients that works. Do you have those things documented? If not, that's your homework. Start by choosing one aspect of what you do to get down on paper as if you had to teach someone else to do it. You can't teach until you have a completely developed scope of the information. Documentation gives you the ability to reflect, to review, to think critically, to understand. When you understand, then you can teach. Once you have one aspect documented, start on the next one…and so on, and so forth until you have it all down.

### Structure in Closing

Whatever you are consistently doing, document it so that you have a full grasp of what your current structure is. When you understand your current structure, you can add to it or subtract from it. Then the rest of this book becomes even more useful. More importantly, your training product becomes even more consistent—saving you head space and improving your clients' experience.

Transitioning, let's take the discussion to an often misunderstood and misapplied aspect of guidance—accountability.

### Accountability

Accountability is an often-used word that's often ill-defined—creating a chasm between how it should facilitate action and the reality of how people use it. It's perceived as if it is, or should be, some kind of finger wagging—a disappointed mother giving out a "tisk, tisk" to a naughty child. When viewed this way, accountability feels kind of weird...it's guilt-and shame-based. (Which at some level we have guilt and shame programmed into us for a reason. This just isn't totally the right context.) Throughout my career, I've seen how unproductive this type of "accountability" is. No one ends up feeling good about it—even the coach. Unless the coach is a complete sociopath that gets off on holding other people down.

In the coaching style that we practice at my gym and in Strength Faction, accountability is a process driven by the clients' wanting and aiming buttressed by the support of structure and coaching. It's not one of accountability based totally on avoiding disappointment or disapproval. There will, however, always be an element of avoiding disappointment and disapproval—we are human. We want to be accepted, and we don't want to let other people down—patterns of social behavior older than we can fathom that aren't going anywhere any time soon. It isn't necessarily a bad thing, wanting to be accepted while avoiding disappointing others, it's just a thing—a part of how we function. There's only a problem when we lean too heavily on that part of us. It becomes destructive—for the client and the coach.

For us, accountability is about personal commitment and relationships. We help our clients settle on the thing, or things, they want to commit to—and alongside them, we formulate a path to achieve that thing. Something meaningful. Something purposeful. Something that can survive motivation's low tide, because low tides inevitably come. Folks need to understand that low tide is coming, that it's normal, and that the right kinds of commitments will see them through it.

This process of commitment and action is enveloped by a healthy relationship. Accountability doesn't work if two people can't level with each other, be honest, and, maybe most importantly, sincerely want to be around each other. It's especially true in the private coach-client setting. A disliked boss may be able to hold someone accountable because they have the person's livelihood in their hands, but we don't wield that kind of power. (I'll also hazard to say that kind of accountability is a poor long-term strategy even in the work place. People will eventually resist in one way or another.) The best accountability tool is a healthy relationship with the person that's asking you for help.

So, what do we do to be an accountability source? How do we help foster those commitments and use our relationship to help folks stay on track? There are four simple elements that we can blend together to become, and remain, solid accountability sources for our clients.

**Have Your Own Accountability System**

Every other Thursday morning at 7:30am sharp, I meet my mentor Bill Hartman on a ZOOM conference call. For half an hour we chat. Bill asks me questions about the big things that I'm currently working on, we check in on the progress I'm making with my goals, and we project forward by setting objectives for the next two weeks until we meet again. Most importantly, he makes sure that I'm taking care of myself—something I've lapsed on in the past. And he gives me sound advice sponsored by his rich life experience.

I sought Bill out for a couple of reasons. There was a void I needed to fill. Between Strength Faction, our members at the gym, and our coaches at the gym, I'm an accountability source to a lot of people, but I didn't have anyone checking in on me. That's a lot of energy going out without much replacing going on—and as we fill other's buckets, we have to replenish our own. If I didn't fill that void, and gain a mentor to check in on me, I'd end up drained and unfocused. And a drained, unfocused coach is of no use to anyone.

Along with the awareness of needing mentorship, I knew that I needed a mentor that I had profound respect for. First and foremost, Bill Hartman is a good man. There is nothing that I've ever witnessed of Bill that causes me to question his integrity or his intentions. And Bill's goodness is bolstered by his intellect. Not only is Bill a great dude, he's probably the smartest dude in the fitness industry. He's the kind of guy I'd like to be when I'm in my fifties. The kind of guy I'd like to be led by. I knew I needed a guy like him or I wouldn't listen as intently as I should. As you consider your own mentorship needs, think about what type of person you'd need to gel with as an accountability source. It's an important piece of the puzzle.

Having Bill check in on me lifts some weight off of my shoulders. His guidance helps me get clear on what I need to do to make my priorities actionable realities. He helps me focus and he helps me plan. That clarity saves me energy and helps me feel in control, and it gives me the resources that help others do the same. Besides Bill, I have two other tools in my accountability system—our team at the gym and my planner.

At BSP NOVA, we help each other set and achieve individual goals. Using our Table of Stable Growth, we set goals in four areas of our lives. We break them down by year, and by quarter, and we check in with each other's progress at least bi-weekly during our staff inservices. We have to show up ready to talk about what we did, or did not do, to make progress toward our goals during the time that's elapsed. If one of us has struggled, the team pulls together to help think through solutions so that whoever is having a rough go of it can overcome the obstacles. Knowing that we are supported, but also have to show up and talk about the moves we're making to a team of people that cares about us, is a huge accountability source.

The simplest tool in my accountability system is my planner. Having a written structure gets things out of the head and allows for visualization. Lay it down on paper, see it in the mind's eye and lay the course of a day or week—it makes action much clearer. In the words of my main man, Chris Merritt, clarity is a hell of a drug. There's also magic in writing something down. Once pen hits paper, things become real and, at least in my case, that builds a level of self-accountability.

All of these accountability tools are great, and helpful, but they are fruitless without truly directing yourself toward goals based on a future that you value. My conversations with Bill are always insightful, but that insight lends itself because I've actually articulated what it is that I want and why I'm working to achieve it. The same goes for the team check-ins and for my planner. If all of your accountability efforts aren't supported by a foundation of high-value outcomes that you seriously want, then it's just a list of nice things that you do, not an accountability system.

This is all to drive home the point that accountability rests within the individual. Knowing that we may have to report our actions can drive us to act positively, but if we aren't sincerely connected to the what and why of our actions, then no person can hold us to them. Having people to check in on us, and a system for tracking
is important, but if we don't ultimately value the future that we're acting towards check-ins and tracking

won't matter. Accountability is an internal, individual responsibility.

Once we have our own accountability handled, we can help others. And, as mentioned above, it begins with the relationship.

**Maintain the Relationship**

People don't want help from people they are having beef with, and accountability works best when two people share a solid connection. For those reasons, we have to do one, simple thing—value the relationship above all else.

Keep in mind one of the big three reasons that people seek fitness coaching—to feel human connection. The connection, and the relationship that maintains it, is individually dependent. Personality, history, and the current context always have to be considered. But if we work to see each person through their individual lens (e.g. Their personality—what, why, how, and other things we know about them), practice unconditional positive regard, and remember our purpose, we keep the coach-client relationship healthy and intact. And if we do that, *then* we can start talking about accountability.

The reality is that you won't become friends with all of your clients, whereas you'll become familial with others. Both situations are fine. But we need connection enough that there's understanding and mutual respect. That's the foundation of accountability. Hell, that's the foundation of everything we do as a coach. But without that foundation, there is definitely no basis for accountability.

## System of Check-ins Based on Goal-Setting and Coaching Structure

Having your own accountability system and maintaining a healthy coach-client relationship are the two big pieces that construct accountability's foundation. Goal-setting, and the check-in structure accompanying it, is the brick and mortar that raises the accountability structure. Setting a purposeful goal, and checking in on it with a coach at predictable intervals, gives a person something worth committing to and something that they can hold themselves accountable to, while also demonstrating to them that they aren't alone in their struggle to succeed—there's someone that cares to check in on them and help them achieve what they want.

Goal-setting and check-ins also allow people to project themselves forward into the future and see incremental progress. It's that incremental progress piece that's huge. Giving folks the opportunity to see that their efforts are taking them places reinforces their belief in their purpose. It's worth reiterating that humans get more out of seeing progress toward a goal than they do actually achieving a goal.

We'll talk about actually creating a goal-setting and check-in structure in our aims and goals section. But, for now, examine your current system. Are you helping people set meaningful goals and employing a system of periodic check-ins that allows them to see progress and hold themselves accountable?

## Honestly Leveling with People and Maintaining Your Own Curiosity

Through the course of the discussion up to this point, it's been clear that accountability is equal parts relationship and structure. Both parts are molded together into process with one, simple medium—honesty. It's honesty from both parties that allows accountability to work—otherwise someone is fooling someone else or two people are fooling themselves and each other.

From our side, the coach's half of the relationship, we have to level with people using a positive, bright realism. Using our best, informed judgement as we put on our coach hat, we give our clients the truth about their current situation, packaged in a way that they'll hear it, while helping them create the transformational plan of action that they can follow. Clients have to level with us about what's truly going on with them.

It all begins, however, with unconditional positive regard—that whole 'recognizing other humans for their being human and letting them be human' thing that we talked about during our discourse on psychological safety. If a person is certain that you're going to judge them, there's a damn good chance that they aren't going to tell you the truth—and they might misconstrue the truth you're attempting to share with them as you being some kind of jerk, perhaps one of Debbie Downer's first cousins, Jack Jerkface. This is a bad thing. Honesty needs trust—and we have to demonstrate, at every possible opportunity, that we have our clients' best interests in mind.

**Here's a scenario to illustrate.**

During an end of phase chat, a female client told me that she'd like to be able to do six, unassisted chin-ups by the end of her next program. At the time of our chat she could only muster two, clean, unassisted chin-ups. I could have been happy-go-lucky, rah-rah, bullshitter and told her, "Awesome! We'll go after that! I believe in you! You can totally do it!" But, I knew that would be totally untrue. Did I totally believe that she could eventually do six clean chin-ups? Absolutely. She wouldn't, however, add four more chin-ups in a month's time with the training and lifestyle schedule she follows. So, I told her that, and we talked.

First, let's be clear that I didn't just make an asshole statement like, "There's no way you'll add four chin-ups in a month. Not going to happen!" I acknowledged and facilitated her desire, and I said something like, "I love that goal, I think six chin-ups is definitely do-able for you. But I think we need to talk time frame." She appreciated the honesty and the way that I packaged it. We went on to figure out an appropriate goal for the next four weeks that fed her bigger goal of getting six, unassisted chin-ups...and all was right with the world.

Because I leveled with her, and gave her a realistic scope, she could maintain a big goal and chunk it down into manageable steps that she could commit to. Without the absolute truth, at some point her efforts would have lost their purpose and potentially turned to futility when she realized that the wasn't working toward a realistic outcome. And there are few things that kill accountability like feeling that our efforts are futile. Honesty frames things appropriately, and realistically, so people can commit to meaningful action.

**Skin in the Game**

There's a sad lesson that I've learned throughout the years—free rarely works. That might be better stated, "free rarely gets people to work." Unless it's upfront offer to cut risk and get people to start training with you, when we totally comp memberships something weird often happens with the person you're trying to help; they don't take full advantage of the gift, and they end up wasting it—causing frustration for the coach and retarding the client's growth.

When people make an investment, however, things change. Putting skin in the game, whether that skin is totally monetary or some other means of exchange, changes the commitment level. I can't totally say why, but an investment raises the stakes. And when the stakes are raised, people value services, and the effort they approach those services with, in a much more serious way. So, while there's a part of me that would love to train everyone for free and financially sustain myself by other means, there's a larger part of me that knows it wouldn't actually be the best thing for most of my clients. They need to have skin in the game.

Having something at stake is a strong accountability source. Look, I know it might seem silly to mention that your clients should feel the hit in their back account for working with you each month, but we fitness coaches tend to be a soft-hearted bunch—and we give too much away for free. And it's not always the best thing for our clients. Payment, having skin in the game, is a powerful source of accountability for people. Let people take advantage of it.

You might read these last few paragraphs and thing, "Shit, I have people pay me a lot of money each month, and it still doesn't hold them accountable." I believe you—we all have those people. But, like most things, accountability isn't one size fits all. The combination of these five steps, in different ratios and forms, it what builds an accountability system. Monetary skin in the game is just one element—and it doesn't always matter. There are other ways for people to put skin in the game.

Purpose and meaning could be part of the exchange. If folks have an emotional investment in training with you, whether you run a gym or are a commercial trainer working at a big box, it's much more likely that they'll feel the necessity to show their face, be a part of something bigger, and train. For example, if you hold regular social events, issue challenges among your clients, and do things together that serve a higher purpose, your clients will feel the emotional investment. And that emotional tie will make them feel connected to you or to your gym. That kind of connection gets people to show up to train because they don't want to lose the other elements that your gym brings to their identity.

For example, we regularly do charitable things with the coaches and clients at our gym. It builds a sense of solidarity and connection between everyone—and it tells the client, rightfully so, that they are the type of person that does charitable things. And their gym mates are the people that they do those things with. That's a sincere emotional investment—a lot of existential skin loaded into the game. It's a source of accountability because it gets people showing up for other people in multiple ways. Clients get to know deeper parts of each other, so they show up to support each other. I don't think there's a better accountability source in the world than feeling that level of connection and support. That's serious skin in the game.

**Facilitating Ownership**

According to self-determination theory (SDT), human beings have three, fundamental psychological needs—*autonomy, competence, and relatedness*. We want to feel as though we can direct our own paths. We want to feel as though we have the skills and knowledge to do the directing, and we want to feel connected to other people as we direct ourselves forward through life's tumults, calms, and transformations. The theory is also founded on the belief that people want to naturally behave in healthful, growth-fulfilling ways. SDT is one of the foundational blocks of our coaching philosophy, and in the context of accountability, all of the basic psychological needs play a serious role.

Autonomy, as it relates to accountability and training, is simple—we facilitate a client's ability to take ownership over their training process. Rather than getting a little too big for our coaching britches and coming from a place of, "I know best, I'm the expert here. Here's the correct answer and just do your program," we function with a more humanistic and client-centered focus. (Remember that whole talk on being the guide and not the hero?) That means that we assume that each person has the ability to choose what's best for themselves under good circumstances and solid guidance. It also means that we take our place as the guide, we put the client in the driver's seat and we serve as the GPS.

Coach curiosity is the first step in facilitating client ownership. It's the simplest way to put the client in the metaphorical driver's seat. We ask more questions. Asking questions does a couple of important, autonomy-supportive things: it communicates to the client that they are capable of directing their own path and that their choices actually hold the answers about what the best next move is, and it gives them the opportunity to express their thoughts and see them evolve to become their training process. Think of it this way, we are a tool box that a client searches through to find the correct tool for the job they are currently working on. Our questions help a client have an inner self-discussion about which tool to choose. Then, they ultimately get to choose that tool.

Context, however, is paramount when it comes to autonomy and helping clients choose the right tool. Yes, people hold the answers to what their next best move is, but they need raw information to be able to sort out the answers. Our clients aren't gym and training content experts. They aren't going to be able to pull the right answers out of thin air. But if we offer them choices, based on what we know about them, their goals, and consistent actions that have demonstrably worked for other people, they can supply themselves with the right answers. Autonomy, in this sense, isn't just being hands off and telling folks to just go with what they feel. It's helping to direct them down a great path and letting them choose how they walk it.

It's absolutely necessary to apply context-driven autonomy to the goal setting process. Buy-in is so crucial, and an autonomy-supportive process promotes that buy-in. And where there's buy-in, there's better accountability. Clients are usually more willing (there are always exceptions) to hold themselves to commitments that they've chosen, rather than those dictated to them by someone else— in our case, a coach. Accountability in this process is also the supportive type that we described earlier, rather than the punitive-feeling type that we're so used to thinking of. That's autonomy-driven accountability. Competency, and the feelings of capability that it engenders, helps bind feelings of autonomy with concrete action.

Earlier into this foray of all things fitness coaching, we had a great, general discussion on competency. Let's slide the lens of accountability over it and view it a bit more specifically.

People want to feel like they know what they're doing, and when they feel like they don't, or can't grasp just what in the hell is going on, it messes with them. That "mess" often ends up with a person feeling demotivated to show up and work, and strongly motivated to avoid the environment that is making them feel incompetent. To draw on an earlier example, if a person feels as though they have no idea how to strike up a casual conversation in a social setting, they'll likely avoid showing up to parties. And a lot of accountability rests on the willingness to show up.

If folks feel woefully incompetent, and without a visible path to competency, as they train with you it's going to be damn tough to hold them accountable because they won't show up—or at least not in the way that is most productive for their growth. Feelings of competency, or at least seeing one's ability to obtain it, motivate people to keep trying their hand. Feeling competent motivates people to keep doing the positive things that are changing them for the better. When people feel as though they can handle a situation, even if not completely now but they see a path to mastery, they keep showing up. Showing up consistently, and fighting the daily battles, is what wins the long-term, transformation war. Competency births consistency, and consistency births positive change. That's transformation's healthy family tree.

Fostering competency begins with understanding the person in front of you, and a few simple questions lend that understanding: *Where is this person currently at, and what is their history, with exercise? What's at least a little bit of what makes them tick?* The answers to simple questions like these help us find a person's starting and/or current level—as well as how they view themselves, their abilities, and the way they approach learning and challenging situations. Your movement screen and initial orientation to your coaching should answer the exercise mastery question. And getting to know the person through casual conversations as well as with questions on your intake form, like 'How would your best friend describe you,' will give an early snapshot of what makes him or her tick.

Using this info, their current movement capabilities and what you know about their personality, match the person with the appropriate level of exercise complexity and training difficulty. What, you ask, is the appropriate level of exercise complexity and training difficulty? Well, it's individually dependent, of course! The appropriate level, the sweet spot of competency, is when a person feels as though they have skill enough to perform the exercises on their program but there's enough challenge to make it interesting. Sometimes the challenge comes from the complexity of the exercise itself—learning, and performing, the movement takes a fair deal of concentration an effort. Other times the challenge comes from loading an easy exercise in a difficult way. Maybe the person doesn't have incredible movement capabilities, but they can perform a basic goblet squat well. The goblet squat, and their ability to proficiently perform it, allows them to demonstrate their competency. The difficult loading scheme, say slow eccentrics, provides the interesting challenge.

Each human is different in how they perceive their own competence and the level of challenge they're willing to take on. That's why it's so important to learn as much as possible about clients to individualize not only the combination of exercises and volume on their program, but their training experience as a whole. When a person lands in their competence sweet spot, there's a better chance that they'll take ownership over their training process, and ownership is the absolute crux of accountability. Relatedness, then, wraps autonomy and competence in a warm embrace of human connection that further motivates a client to keep showing up.

Relatedness is the relationship building aspect that we've discussed—it's being a human being that treats other human beings like human beings. When we do this, people want to be around us, and, as we mentioned, there's no accountability between a client and a coach that don't want to be around each other. Relatedness is a simple reminder that relationship is at the forefront of everything.

The combination of autonomy, competence, and relatedness meets a person's basic psychological needs, and in doing that, fosters a sense of ownership. Ownership that's truly felt, through self-direction, feelings of ability, connection to something bigger, and connection to others is the absolute embodiment of accountability.

## *Accountability in Closing*

Accountability isn't as simple as some old-school, toe-the-line, hard-ass philosophy in action. It's much more nuanced than that—especially in our realm where adults are choosing to ask other adults for help. It starts, and is totally enveloped, by relationship. If people want to be around you, it's much more likely that they'll show up and, in turn, do the things that they need to do for themselves. Developing a structure that gives people the means to set realistic goals that they actually want to commit to, that's reinforced with consistent follow up, keeps people focused. Making sure that people are properly invested with skin in the game ups the ante. And understanding that ownership is the pinnacle of accountability, and how the tenets of self-determination theory foster ownership, is the keystone that supports the arch of accountability.

You, and your leadership, is the glue that binds the connections of the arch. You're a sacred type of glue, one that has their own accountability sources and is truly living an accountable life so that you may pass that on to your clients. Sure, accountability begins and ends with the client taking ownership, but you are the glue that holds their system of accountability together. You are the guide that shows them the path that leads to the transformation on the other side of ownership. Take that seriously. Own your accountability and give your clients the information they need, in a way they need to hear it, so that they may own theirs.

## *Teaching*

"Bone 22."

I can't tell you how many times I walked into a huddle during my high school football career and said that to my teammates. It probably isn't that hard to figure out, but I'm not a statistician, so I don't know that kind of shit. Being that, for most of my career, I was a quarterback in a wishbone option offense, I can promise you that it was a lot.

There are times that I can still feel a sharp, cool Autumn breeze drying the sweat on the back of my neck. The sounds of the hometown stands filled with the cheers of parents, the war chant song of the high school band, and the support of the cheerleaders still echo through my ears as if they were just now bursting through the sound holes in my helmet. The defense is aligned in front of me as I approach the line of scrimmage, staring confidently at the middle linebacker, knowing that I'm about to make him look like a fool.

Blazing hot practices in the dead of August's dog days are still imprinted clearly on my memory as well—not just the emotion and pageantry of game days. As I write this, I see the dust kicking up on the summer scorched practice field behind what used to be Highland Park Elementary School—it's since been closed, a victim of school consolidations. There we are, all of us in our white practice jerseys and our black helmets, drilling the elements of each play that we'll eventually run smoothly as a unit. We're learning our defensive roles, how to adjust to different offenses, how to employ the fundamentals in a game situation.

These are the things you'd almost expect a guy to remember fifteen years after he played his last snap of high school football—the emotional images, the reminders of days gone by, the mental transportation of place and time and a fond remembrance of things that at one time felt like a struggle. The crazy thing is, I still remember everything that's supposed to happen during "Bone 22", a triple option play that was the staple of our offense.

Like the visions of hot, exhausting August days, the rules of the play are still imprinted on my memory. I step to ten o'clock as I reach the ball out to mesh with the fullback, and my eyes are on the first man on, or outside the tackle, because he's my first read. If he collapses toward our mesh, I pull the ball and run, and the second man on or outside the tackle is my read for the pitch. If he commits to me, I pitch the ball to the half-back and let him do his thing. But I don't just remember my role, I remember what everyone else is supposed to do, too. I won't bore you with all of the details, because we'd be here for a while, but it's all still there. The blocking assignments, and the accompanying rules, what the half-back opposite the play is supposed to do, where the tight end releases to. It's all still there.

At first thought, it seems crazy that after fifteen years, a college football career, lots of knocks on the noggin, and a lot of life lived, that I can remember all this. But, in reality, it's no mystery. My coach, Pennsylvania legend, Gawen Stoker, had an unsurpassed knack for taking obnoxious amounts of information and condensing it down into easy to remember rules and actions. He was a master of transferring information, of teaching.

"Bone 22" is just one, small example, but it's an expressly illustrative one. When an offensive player on Coach Stoker's teams heard that play called, all of the rules and actions were implied and understood. There were no convoluted miss-mashes of words to make things more complicated than they needed to be. "Bone 22" means this...now go and do it. All of the potentialities were accounted for in the simplest of rules, and it was all communicated with one word and a number. Bone, the formation, and 22, the series of play and the area where the play would be carried out. It was simplistically, profoundly, brilliant.

That's our job as fitness coaches—to educate our clients, to transfer our knowledge to them in a simply profound way that they easily express through their movements, their mindsets, and their lifestyles. In a style reminiscent of Coach Stoker's, we teach movement in an understandable way that loads a ton of information into a small package—and we individualize to the person as much as necessary. We educate in a way that takes the insane complexity of fitness and nutrition information, combines it with simple lifestyle habits, and condenses it into digestible chunks, slathered with context that helps a client actually understand and use it.

The main, and most important way that we teach our clients is through direct, on-the-floor coaching. We'll introduce and dissect the four-part coaching paradigm that I created in 2014 and have since implemented
with all of our BSP NOVA coaches, taught around the world, and introduced to Strength Faction. It nails on the floor coaching. Combining elements of psychology, basic information chunking, and environment, it amalgamates into an everyday coaching practice that will revolutionize how you teach your clients.

## Direct Coaching

Your knowledge is literally expressed through movement in someone else's body. That's wild to think about, isn't it? A bit of information that you know travels through whatever means of teaching that you're employing and is expressed in the action of another human. It's incredibly cool. How you transfer that information from your brain to the person that needs it, in a way that they can actionably understand, is...well, that's skilled coaching.

And skilled coaching is the product of attentive repetitions. We need simple, every day guides to help us direct our actions while also focusing our attention so that we may self-evaluate, learn more about the person we are coaching, and think critically about the outcomes of our interventions. Our four-part coaching paradigm is designed to meet those ends—guide your actions so that you help each client in the right way and focus your attention, so you can continually improve your skills.

We'll take a brief overview of the paradigm and then discuss each constituent part individually.

# The Coaching Paradigm

*Following this coaching paradigm has deepened our connections with our clients, helped us build a stronger gym community, and, ultimately, helped our clients achieve better results. Here are the four parts:*

1. Find the bright spots: tell them what they're doing well first
2. Clearly identify problems. Communicate this using the least amount of info possible.
3. Cue in context
4. Dramatically reinforce positive change

## Find the Bright Spots

Starting with positive statements keeps people from clamming up and opens them to the coaching your about to give. It's simple psychology—most people are much more apt to listen if you don't jump right down their throats with everything that they did incorrectly. People want to be seen and they need their efforts acknowledged.

Start with a negative comment, or immediately jump into corrections and they are more apt to close up and not accept your coaching. Besides, it's rare that a client does everything completely wrong.

Here are a few examples of well-constructed opening comments...

> *"I like the way you did X, that looked really good, let's work on..."*
>
> *"You did a great job with X, that was great, what if..."*
>
> *"Nice job with X! Let's build on that, how about..."*

These are, of course, conversations that occur between sets or between exercises.

## Clearly Identify Problems, Communicate Succinctly

This starts with the Gestalt to Fault coaching approach. See the whole movement, the pattern, so that you can narrow focus and find idiosyncrasies.

Clearly identifying problems, then, starts with having a grasp on the movement you're coaching. We must constantly strive to deepen our understanding of movement to better understand what we are looking for. To communicate the problem, however, understand that less information is better.

The client is already working to process information sent to the brain by their body, and their conscious attempts to move. This takes up space in working memory. Add your language to the equation and you start to crowd the processor. Feedback, then, must be short and sweet. No more than a couple of words, and only attempting to address one, or maybe two, movement issues.

For now, let's illustrate an example of clearly identifying an exercise execution issue and a succinct coaching intervention.

A client isn't sitting back enough when they squat. You let them complete the rep they're on, so not to crowd their processor, and then simply state, "sit back." You notice that this client's knees are also caving as they squat, but you don't address both problems at the same time. You wait until the next rep and then cue them to "spread."

In this example you've clearly identified two problems but addressed them separately to not give the client too much information at once. You've also used succinct speech in order to limit the information the client must process while completing an exercise.

A few quick guidelines:

- Never address more than two issues at once. In most instances address only one. Fix the next issue during the next rep. In some instances, wait until the next set.

- When correcting an issue only give the clients one or two bits of info.

- Use as few words as possible.

If addressing issues between sets, be mindful of the same guidelines but it's ok to elaborate a bit more on what you're seeing. But keep it short and sweet. Here's an example: "You did a great job spreading the floor, what if you tried sitting back more when you squat, right now you're dropping straight down and it's shooting you forward. If you sit back more so your hips will have more room to move."

## Cue in Context

External coaching cues instruct clients to accomplish a movement task without drawing attention to specific body parts in a performance environment. This keeps clients focused on execution rather than thinking too intently on what certain body parts are doing, limiting confusion. This concept follows the same thought line as communicating succinctly. We're limiting the amount of information, and the type of information, a client must process at one time.

Here are some tangible examples:

When cueing a person during the up phase of a hip hinge exercise (deadlift, rack pull, trap bar deadlift, etc.) make driving the floor away the focus point. The goal is to coordinate hip and knee action, but mentioning the hips, knees or, any muscles associated with each, limits performance. Using a cue such as "drive the floor away" instead keeps people moving without consciously trying to identify their body parts and what they're doing. Hip and knee extension is efficiently coordinated.

When cueing hip torque while squatting, again draw attention to the floor. Cue the client to "spread the floor" or "tear the floor in half." This gets them to spread their knees and create hip external rotation torque that produces tension and strength. Mentioning the knees or the hips in this instance causes the client to think about their body instead of just moving.

Learning environments, however, sometimes require internal cues that draw attention to body parts, often in combination with tactile cues.

Let's illustrate with a hypothetical story.

You have a new client that's woefully unaware of his body. He's an office worker that's never participated in anything athletic and you're his first gym experience. He doesn't even have a rudimentary understanding of how his body moves and how it should feel while it moves. At this point in his training process he needs to internalize what different body segments feel like when they work so that he may integrate them into healthy, performance-based movements as he progresses in his training. For example, he needs to feel his spine move and understand that's different from his hips moving. Often the best way to give a person that understanding is to draw attention to the spine, and name it, as the person attempts to move it. Then attention is drawn to the hip, glutes, whatever, as the person learns to move that segment of their body.

As the client gains context and understanding, external, performance-based cues become more useful.

## Dramatically Reinforce Positive Change

Humans are emotional beings—we change most often because emotion goads us to change. Emotional events are also tied much stronger to memory. Think of something you did successfully in your life, you most likely remember it more clearly than mundane day-to-day activities.

Apply that to our fitness coaching context. We celebrate success emphatically! (Note the exclamation point.)

Let's use a brief illustration.

You've been coaching an athlete as she rack pulls. She's had trouble with coordinating her hips and knees—shooting her knees under the bar, and scooping up, rather than extending her hips and knees simultaneously. Then, on set three, she gets it! She "drives the floor away" and does five perfect reps. You respond with "Yes! That's exactly it! You did a great job." Or something along those lines. The keys are your tone of voice, facial expression and body language.

This type of input communicates a couple of things to the client. First, that you care about her and are happy for her success. This helps her generate future motivation to just want to be around you. Second, it creates a memorable environment. She'll be more likely to remember how to rack pull because you created an environment in which it's easier for her to remember what she did correctly.

## Going Deep on the Paradigm

Alright, we're armed with a paradigm overview and the basics of action. Now we're going to go deeper on each pillar of the paradigm and talk more specifically about application. As always, we'll start with the bright spots.

## Note the Bright Spots First

Here's a fact you didn't know about yourself: you're a conversational neurochemist. During your daily coaching interactions, as you attentively and purposefully speak with your clients, you're constantly inciting experiments on how to best influence their neurochemistry. Your words combine with the neuroendocrine system in the cerebral cortex and produce a hormonal result. Every time you coach, your words and deeds can affect your clients' cortisol and oxytocin.

Comments and conversations that evoke negative emotions raise can cortisol levels. When our words make people feel criticized, judged or afraid, it does some nasty things to the brain and body. Cortisol isn't great in our conversational context. If you were trying to survive on a desert island with limited food, it's a good thing. But given that we're helping folks improve their bodies and lives, we should help them keep that cortisol down.

So, what happens when cortisol increases due to feeling negatively about a conversation? Less resources are allocated to the parts of our brain that think, and more are given to those choose between fight and flight. Rather than being calm, calculated thinkers, we devolve into increasingly sensitive and reactionary beings—we perceive more judgment than is really happening. But wait, there's more! This negative hormonal environment can last for more than a day—affecting people long after they leave our coaching sessions.

Positive conversations, or at least the perception of positive conversations, increase oxytocin levels—the "feel good" hormone that helps us feel compassion, act generously, and bids us to cooperate with others. (Perception is the key. Some folks perceive a difficult conversation positively whereas others take it as unbearably negative and soul crushing.) It also can help us remember things, especially patterns and social cues. Which are important in a socially-based learning environment like a training gym. Unfortunately, its effects don't last as long as cortisol. The oxytocin button must be pressed more often for lasting effects.

Remember, whether you like it or not, you're a conversational neurochemist. You can use your words to release the kraken of cortisol, or to press the oxytocin button in the name of cooperation. This isn't an argument for growing overwhelmingly soft, shedding your backbone, and turning into a doormat that only says nice things all the time. It is, rather, a call to pause and consider that how we handle conversations, especially ones that will necessarily be critical, so that we may positively affect our clients. Perception is key, and beginning with bright spots, while tempering them with a consideration of the person in front of you and your relationship with them, often shapes a conversation that holds a necessarily critical element into one that a client perceives positively. What actions can we take to foster that positive perception?

## *Start with Effort*

In her book, *Mindset*, Carol Dweck describes the importance of reinforcing effort for building resiliency and defeating learned helplessness in the folks that we guide—whether we are teaching, coaching, parenting, etc. Acknowledging effort makes it valuable—and people that want to do well in any social context align their behavior with what is perceived as valuable. Recognizing folks with bright spots such as, 'you're great at that, or you're a good so-and-so', while still positive, and potentially useful dependent on the context, doesn't have as big of an impact on helping people build consistent, positive action. It doesn't help them grow as persevering, resilient, transformative people. Those kinds of comments offer a minute finality to a person—the task is done, you are what you could become in this area. Consistently speaking to a person that way makes being acknowledged for a perceptively static identity the value worth seeking. Rather than expressing effort in the name of transformation, it says 'you've done all the work you needed to do.' Allow me to preach to the choir for just a second and reiterate something echoed for centuries—the work is never done. Knowing that the work is never done, we have to create an environment that reinforces the value of doing the work.

Beyond this, we have to consider the practicality of keeping things positive when it looks as though we have an exercise catastrophe on our hands. Even if a movement looks like a train wreck, and you're having a hard time finding a bright spot, reinforcing effort keeps the door of positivity open so that we can make a productive coaching intervention.

This is, of course, individually dependent and bright spots exist on a spectrum. To some folks, getting kicked the real deal, no matter how bluntly critical it is, is a bright spot. Their bright spot is knowing exactly what they did wrong, so they can make an effort to fix it. Often times you'll find that What people behave this way. We have a client at BSP NOVA that's a great illustration. During one of our monthly challenges, he stated his time and asked how everyone else was doing. When Chris gave him a "bright spot" and said that his time was pretty good, the client responded that, "he wasn't a millennial and didn't need things sugar-coated." It was funny to us, especially since Chris and I are millennials and we don't need any sugar-coating.

Some folks live at the other end of the spectrum. If you're blunt with them, they crumble, perceive the entire deal negatively, and cast you as the villain that hurt their feelings. These are often How people, and they need brighter bright spots first or they'll clamshell on you faster than you can say "Dolly Parton!" This is an example of why it's so important to guide them toward self-reinforcement and peer reinforcement, like ASAP.

Most folks, however, fall somewhere in the middle of the spectrum. Noting even a little bright spot shows them that they were noticed, and it opens them up to appreciating the critical element of your coaching that follows. It's important to keep in mind that how you approach bright spots with a given client will likely evolve over time. Usually, the progression I see is that folks like, and require, more bright spots at the beginning of a coaching relationship, depending on personality, of course. But as they get to know, like, and trust you more, they grow sure of your good intentions—making them generally more open to your coaching. The client realizes that you aren't just there to berate them and show them how wrong they are. Bright spots, however, especially those centered on effort, never totally go out of style.

Appreciating, and noting, effort as an initial bright spot is a great way to positively affect our clients, on many levels, when it seems as though an entire movement went to hell in a handcart, and we're having a hard time finding something to reinforce.

## *What If...*

Ok, let's say that you found an exercise bright spot and you want to announce that sucker to your client. What's a good strategy for leading with the bright spot and then following that up with some coaching? Asking a question.

Here's an example:

> *"Barbara! I loved how you set up for that rack pull. Your hips were in a great position. What if we tried something along with that next set? How about trying to dial our feet harder and set a harder grip on the bar? It seemed like you lost a little tension as you lifted, doing those things will help you keep it."*

Asking a question rather saying, 'that was good, but' facilitates autonomy by involving the client in the coaching process. Barbara is deciding to dial her feet harder and set a better grip, she's not being told to do it. There are times to give directive instructions, and some people prefer it, but any time we can lead with questions and give a client a choice is usually a good thing.

### What Did You Like?

Here's another example that works well with folks that have a few sessions with you under their belt—

simply asking them what they liked about the set after stating your bright spot.

> *"Barb! I loved the tension that time. That was killer. What did you like about that set? Yea? I totally agree. Is there anything you'd like to improve during the next set?"*

Again, Barb is involved in the process of solving her problems rather than being dictated to and the overall feel of the interaction is more positive. She's allowed to evaluate the set and determine what she'd like to do (remember the talk on giving How people the opportunity to reinforce themselves?). Here's the deal, we have to create context and lay the foundation with good cueing before this is possible. People need to understand the difference between good and bad before they're able to answer these questions and coach themselves. Building context early on in the coaching process is pivotal to transition folks to this type of coaching. That's not to say all of your coaching efforts need to be entirely declarative in the early going, but they do need to be devoutly educational.

It starts with letting the first rep suck, and then reinforcing the effort of that first rep while back ending it with some information about how to improve—problem, and solution, slathered in oxytocin.

### It's All Context

Using bright spots is context-based, and perception is the most important factor. Two people often react differently to the same conversations. That's why it's so important to get to know your people, their lives, their motivations, and their backgrounds. What some folks perceive as positive and life-affirming, others perceive as being babied or patted on the ass. We have to pay attention and determine what a bright spot is for each client. There will be a lot of cross over, most people like to hear nice things about themselves. But understanding how to use positives so they fit the person is super-important. It's a simple matter of observation followed by experimentation and then another observation without an attachment to the outcome. Pay attention and learn how to interact with each individual you coach.

### *It's Not Just for Clients; It's for Us, Too*

Coaches seem to be inherent fixers with a pervasive malady—hammer and nail syndrome. We want to find the problems and hammer those sons-a-bitches. But that often puts us in the wrong mindset of being on a constant seek and destroy mission rather than maintaining the positivity that helps us create a growth-oriented environment. Finding the bright spots first helps us develop a "good-first" mindset that influences everything about how we coach our people, run our businesses, and live our lives. It's much easier to be a calculated conversational neurochemist when we aren't totally focused on everything that's wrong.

## *After the Bright Spots*

After searching for the bright spots and finding them, communication is everything. I offered some conversational notes in this section, but let's move on to coaching in real time and have a discussion on how to know what we are looking for and communicate that succinctly. It'll help us avoid overwhelming our clients with information.

## Clearly Identify, Communicate Succinctly

I closed the conversation on bright spots by mentioning that we're inherent fixers. We love to see a problem, offer an intervention, and see the positive outcome. Sometimes, however, it makes us verbose and overbearing—we say too much, and we try to correct too much. And, sometimes, as we offer those corrections we don't even have a clear objective in mind. We just need to fix something to prove our value to ourselves and to our clients. It's an immature thought process that we need to eliminate... and using this pillar of the paradigm is a practical way to squash it.

It begins with some upfront work—defining our movements, knowing our cues, creating the right environment, and understanding the person in front of us. But that work pays coaching dividends tenfold.

### *Movement Definitions*

We all have an idea of a squat is and thoughts on how to cue it, but can you define a squat and what it should look like to you? What should move—when and where? What should be still—when and where? It might sound like a pain in the ass, but writing this out, and defining the squat for yourself, improves your ability to clearly identify what you're looking for in the moment that you're coaching. You can, with quick, concise precision, tell if everything is spot on, or if something looks slightly askew. You can move from Gestalt to Fault much faster.

The ability to clearly articulate to ourselves, and write down what something should look, like enhances our ability to visualize it in the moment because as we write our definition we have to continually visualize a good and a bad movement as we pen every line. We become absolutely sure of what we want, and how to modify
for individuals, in a super hurry. We've done all the thinking up front, so we don't have to think as much in the moment.

So, here's what to do:

Pull out the list of all the main movements in your training rolodex and define them. Start with the big guys—the squat, the hinge, the push, the pull—and then, on a needs basis so that you're working with context, define the rest of your movement rolodex. What should move—where and when? What should stay still? Where should the body, and its accompanying parts, be positioned—how and why? It's going to take time and effort, but you'll have much better identification skills for it.

### Create the Environment

Let's pause for a hot second to consider the things affecting a client's brain as they perform an exercise under your supervision. They're sending efferent information down the chain to get their body to move, and often times they have to be more cognitive about it than you or I do. Afferent information is coming back from their sensory system to tell them just where their body is in space. There's motivation to do the exercise correctly—partly to please themselves, partly to please you, and partly to not look like a fool in front of other people in the gym. Also, a light just flickered, someone coughed, the floor feels weird under their left food, and that guy in the short-shorts that makes the sex moans while he does biceps curls just walked in.

The combination of the client's internal and the external environment puts a lot on the ol' processor when they're performing a movement. This is especially true in the early going when he or she is learning a movement. We have to take all of this into consideration, and then, rather than indiscriminately using our words, we use them as tools.

Speak as little as possible, using only the necessary words, to improve someone's movement—making sure those words pertain to the current context. (Context, context, context...there it is a few more times just in case you haven't read it enough. But it's important, so keep reading it. Oh, and there's an entire section on it coming up. Hooray!) Most of your heavy talking work is done in the early going of working with a client. It's a learning environment—so the client must think more, and we have to give them the context in which to think. Hence our words. This is when we introduce the cues that they can internalize, and it's when we deepen their understanding of the movements and their outcomes. We create an internal environment that allows them to coach themselves. That way, in the moment when they're performing, we only have to give them brief reminders—using the coaching mantras—or have a context-filled discussion between sets.

Once folks have context and understanding, communication then becomes succinct, and takes place mainly internally for the client. The goal is always to prepare clients to coach themselves and create the input that helps them understand. Some folks are visual, and others are more kinesthetic. Some are auditory, but need the information in small chunks and between action. No matter the input, the outcome is to create the internal environment that allows people to coach themselves. That's how they ascend toward mastery.

Rather than hearing us blabber on about how to perform a moment, our clients often learn better in an environment that teaches good bodily position and movement performance. While we'll never totally remove our need to verbally cue our clients, finding ways to create an environment that cues them without our words facilitates movement learning in a way that often helps people "get it" faster. I'd be remiss not to offer examples.

A lot of folks struggle with excessive torso lean when they are learning to squat. Rather than staying upright at the torso and sitting into their hips, they end up doing a squat-good morning hybrid and pop locking it to stand up. Not so bad if you're sweating it up on the dance floor (Pop lock and drop it. Pop lock and drop it. You're welcome for putting that into your head for the rest of the day.), but definitely bad for building a loadable squat. Two drills I really dig for creating an environment that keep folks out of pop lock land are the plate squat and the bottoms up kettlebell front squat.

Plate squats have a person press a light plate—five or ten pounds—straight out from their chest, holding their arms parallel, as they squat to the depth that works for them. Pressing the plate out and keeping the arms parallel to the floor gives the torso the stimulus to stay upright.

Bottoms up kettlebell front squats ask a lady or gent to hold two kettlebells in the bottoms up position while squatting. Keeping the kettlebells upright requires the person to position their upper-body directly over their hips and, voila, the torso stays upright.

The beauty of these two drills is they don't require any language for the client to "get it." They create an environment. Every coach needs a toolbox filled with these kinds of drills.

## Let the First Rep Suck...Only Make One Change

It's often a *good* thing when a client makes a movement mistake in the early going. But it's also often that we let our inherent fixer open up its mouth and make a correction way too soon. We have to tell that part of ourselves to shut up. Letting the first rep suck gives folks an understanding of what bad feels like which makes it easier for them to find the contrast—what good feels like. It fast tracks their understanding of the movement while helping them to internalize it. As a result, it becomes easier for them to coach themselves. The caveat, however, is safety. If someone is likely to get hurt, then we intervene. But, if it just looks like a less than stellar rep, let it ride. If you've done a good job building context up to that point, you follow up with a quick intervention between the reps—a concise verbal cue, a quick kinesthetic cue, something else you've developed to intervene. Then, after the change is made and the set completed, follow up with a question. Something like,

"What did you like about that set?" Then after that answer, contrast using something like, "Did you feel how what you liked contrasted with the first rep?" By letting the first rep suck, giving a small cue between reps, and then following up with questions, you helped the client coach himself or herself in the future.

We also must patiently make only one change at a time. Trying to change an entire movement during one set is not only unrealistic, it's overwhelming for the client. Use your Gestalt to Fault process, find your big-ticket item, and attack that. It might clear up the whole movement. If it doesn't, move on to the next priority down the chain between the next reps or after the set. If we can change one thing per set, or rep, by the end of a training session we can overhaul an entire movement. We just have to turn down the volume knob on the inherent fixer yelling in our head and be patient.

### The Identification and Communication Rundown

Define your movements. Sharpen your Gestalt to Fault skills.

Teach a lot up front in the learning environment so you don't have to talk as much when clients are performing.

Let the first rep suck.

Cue one change between reps or sets.

Follow up with questions so that clients can internalize the contrast between good and bad.

# Cue in Context

Context is king—that statement applies to all facets of life. Applying understanding to a given situation in the correct way is the crux of success.

The key is thinking in terms of situations rather than broad, sweeping catch-alls. This is especially true for coaching movement. We have to understand the context of what's happening and what the situation needs from us. We must also understand how to create context for our clients so that they understand what's being asked of them.

Let's talk about that in terms of coaching the hinge as we consider different cueing environments.

### *External Cueing, Internal Cueing, and Context*

Let's begin with simple, actionable definitions.

External cues direct attention away from the body and toward an external object with the aim of improving performance. "Spread the floor," is a common external cue to improve positioning and increase hip drive during squat and deadlift variations. Internal cues, in contrast, draw attention to a body part.

Rather than saying, spread the floor, to get the hips working, we'd say something like "spread your knees."

During the past few years external cueing's been heralded while the industry's poo-poo'd internal cueing. There's been a collection of great research that's demonstrated external cueing's superiority in performance situations. So, before considering cueing in multi-dimension, we, collectively, thought unilaterally—jumping on the external bandwagon and hoofing internal cues in the pants. I think we've overreacted.

Here's an admission: I used to be an external cueing Nazi. It was all external cues all the time. I based a part of my coaching paradigm, which I've since changed, on consistent, never-failing external cueing. I was wrong.

I, like most of the industry, failed to consider context. The context of different situations—whether or not clients had the context they needed to understand what was being asked of them and integrate an external cue. I was trying to fit every problem to a single
solution rather than individualizing solutions to unique problems.

But as I coached and coached, strictly using external cues, I noticed something. They didn't always accomplish the desired end. It took a few sessions of aggressively beating my head against the wall until I was like, "Uh, hey man, stop being an idiot. This doesn't work all the time. But you're still really handsome and I love you."

Reality is internal and external cues fit into different contexts. To understand where they fit, we start with the question, *are we learning or are we performing?*

## Learning

Consider a client that's woefully disconnected from their body—a mind traversing the earth with little sense of itself in space. They are incredibly kinesthetically unaware. This person needs a lot of physical learning. They need a combination of environmental, positional, and internal cueing so they can learn and integrate what movements feel like. Integrating those feelings allows them to better understand where their body is in space and replicate movements.

Let's play-pretend that we share a client that can't dissociate their hips from their spine; where their hips go, their spine goes—and vice-versa. Before we can effectively use external hip hinge cues, we have to teach them the difference between their hips and their spine.

We start by having them attempt a standing hip hinge. Remember—letting the first rep suck is a good idea. It gives folks the opportunity to feel what shitty feels like—and that creates an important contrast to what good will feel like.

Now that we've done the hip hinge, we ask them, "Did you feel how your back rounded and you bent over rather than hinging at the hips." They're going to say something like, "no." Or a similar word. Then they'll express that they're not sure they know the difference. (They might, however, say yes. That is, indeed, in the realm of possibilities—this is where you say, "Duh, Todd." If that's the case it just makes your job easier. You can say something like, "Great! I'm glad you felt that. That's actually not the best case scenario... "And then continue on with your coaching.)

Now you get to pretend you're a magician.

Explain that you're going to try a few drills that will teach them the difference between their hips and their spine...and ask them if that's cool. They'll be like, "yes." Or something like that.

We start with the simplest of hip awareness drills—the glute bridge. With them lying on their back and knees bent so their feet are in line with their butt cheeks, we ask them to drive their feet through the floor and squeeze their butt like their trying to pinch something between their cheeks. Once they've done a couple of reps, and you can see that their glutes are doing the work, ask them if they feel their butt working. When they say yes, say good, those are your hips. That's where your hips are and that's what it feels like when they're working. But definitely figuring out phrasing that doesn't sound condescending.

Once they've figured out their hips, flip them over into the quadruped position. And I mean physically flip them over. You pick that person up and turn them over. You're the boss.

Please, don't do that. I'm kidding.

Once you have them in quadruped, coach them through the cat-cow (or as my friend Brendan Rearick calls it, the tiger-bison)—using your hands to kinesthetically cue if necessary. Once they start to get the movement, ask something like, "do you feel how that's your spine moving and not your hips?" They'll say something like, "Well, now that you mention it, indeed I do!" Smashing!

Now that you've created context with position and internal cues, return to the hip hinge and work on performance.

### *Performance*

Quick aside before we go on. We're using the hip hinge as an illustration—this process applies to any movement/exercise/etc.

In the majority of cases, your client will now have a better understanding of their body and will be better able to integrate external cues. Now we'll use our hip hinge cue mantra to get them hinging—tall and tight, reach, drive (TRD).

We've shifted from a learning environment to a performance environment. Could we argue that it's still a learning environment? Of course, everything could technically be called a learning environment—attention, however, differs. At this point we're integrating information in the form of action so that they can perform a more complex movement task. If we have to think too much we can't perform as well.

Learning and performance exist on a continuum. One is never completely separate from the other, at least in the gym, but one is dominant over the other depending on the situation.

In a performance environment, we start with external cueing and work backwards. This means first try an external cue. If that doesn't stick, move to some kind of pattern assistance—use some kind of implement, a pole on the spine, etc., to give them input on position and movement. If you're still not getting anywhere, regress position and cue internally.

External cues keep us in the correct brain centers during performance. They direct action rather than initiate thought. Action keeps us in our lower brain centers—allowing for movement and faster reaction without much cognition. Thought directed by internal cues, pulls us into higher brain centers, which are much slower in producing movement. If a person has to think, they slow down—that doesn't work when fluid movement is the goal.

### *External vs. Internal: The Recap*

If you have someone in front of you that's a poor mover, that's terribly kinesthetically unaware, use internal cues until they make better associations between where they are in space and their body. This denotes a strictly learning environment.

If you're in a performance environment, start with external cues and, if the person is struggling with performance, work backwards to a learning environment and internal cues.

Now that we understand environment, let's have a gander inside our cueing toolbox and fit the right types of cues to the right circumstances.

## Cues: The Big Four Types

One of the coolest things about being human, and one that we certainly take for granted, is how dynamically multi-sensory we are—and how quickly we can integrate the information that comes from our senses into a new understanding. Seriously, think about that. Try this brief, little thought experiment—take all of your senses away but one, I don't care which one, how would you gather information and understand the world? It would be a hell of a lot more difficult—you can bet your boots on that!

If we want our coaching to be as effective as possible, we have to create a multi-sensory experience for our clients—and fit that experience to the environment and the individual. While coaching movement, we draw on three, main sensory systems—auditory, visual, kinesthetic (or tactile), and environmental. Each coaching situation usually requires a blend of all three, but when we consider the person we are coaching, and the current environment, there's a sweet spot that applies each in the proper proportion. Type of application—the right kind of demonstration, the right kind of words, and the right kind of physical guidance—is also part of the equation. Let's look at each type of cueing and apply them in the learning and the performance environments for succinct communication that doesn't leave clients scratching their heads and feeling like they're taking a calculus final.

## Verbal Cues

Simple rules the world of cueing internalization. Remember good old Occam's Razor?—the simplest solution tends to be the right one. Well, the simplest cue tends to be the right one. A convoluted series of words that displays how adept of a cunning linguist you are may impress your client. They might comment, "Well, my goodness gracious, does Jane ever know a lot of magical words! I'd love to hear her order ice cream!" But they won't understand a damn thing about what they should do...and if they do get it, it will take them longer.

Speaking isn't always appropriate and verbal cues aren't always the right coaching tool for a given job. But verbal cueing is still, and likely will always be, our main means of coaching. Humans like to talk to each other. And, when used in the right way, verbal cueing is seriously effective. Verbal cues simply need to fit the environ-ment, the context, and the individual. As we mentioned during our chat on succinct communication, our words need to be well-timed and hold a lot of information in small packages. Let's examine verbal cues through the lens of each coaching environment.

Verbal cues in a learning environment are all about creating context around movements and positions to set clients up for future success. Whether the cue is internal or external, as both could be justifiably used in a learning environment, it has to help the client internalize a process for coaching themselves on a given exercise, or during a portion of a given exercise. If a verbal cue isn't designed to do this, well, it's just unnecessary verbal masturbation...and you can do that on your own time.

The first step in verbal cueing is determining what the problem really is, and we can usually narrow it down to three or four potential things—position, movement execution, and lack of understanding or focus.

If it's a positional issue, for example they've lost control of their hips and trunk and slide into either flexion
or extension, our coaches use simple cues that are introduced to a client during their first day in our gym. Those cues are "tall and tight", "macho man", and "sad dog"—the last one we admittedly stole from our friends at Mark Fisher Fitness. Our clients learn these three positions as they are coached on the correct way to hold a plank—because almost every sagittal plane strength movement is a moving plank, with the bench press being a definite exception.

Let's say that a client let themselves get a bit too extended during their deadlift set-up. We'd utter "tall and tight" to draw their attention to the fact that they were popping their chest out like Randy Savage (R.I.P.) after snapping into an Extra Bold Jalapeño SlimJim. An associated cue in that same vein is "get long." Since we've already taken the time to build context and associate these words with positions, just saying them can snap a person in and help them correct their movement. If they don't get it right away, it's never too late to stop a bad set before it begins and have a quick chat with them.

This chat would still use the simple cues that they were introduced to on day one. It would go something like, "So, you're pretty "macho manny" in your set-up right now, do you feel that?" Then they'd answer yes or no. If yes, the conversation continues by asking them what they have to do to get tall and tight. If no, then this is the time to blend in a visual cue. We'll walk through an entire scenario that blends all three in just a bit, but for now, back to the magic of the tongue.

It also may be the time to remove them from the deadlift's performance environment and move them back to a learning environment for a hot sec. They may need a positional refresher as well as some awareness
of their spine in space. Regressing them back to a foundational hip hinging pattern, say a tall-kneeling handcuffed hinge, to draw attention to the hips moving, and a cat-cow to draw attention to the spine. As we use these regressed movements, we actually use

verbal, internal cues. "Do you feel how that's just your hips moving and not your spine? Do you feel mostly your spine moving there?" Then we bring back in the positional cues—tall and tight, macho man, and sad dog—and associate them with their appropriate positions in each regressed movement.

With a fresh, new load of context dumped on their brains, they return to the barbell to set up for their deadlift set. This is the time when we have to sharpen our coaching vision. If the set-up doesn't improve and put them in a position to be successful during the exercise, you get one more crack at cueing them into a better position. Then, that's it. It's our cueing rule of three.

*We get three chances to cue someone into a better position, and if we can't do it in three attempts we have to change the movement, or the starting position of the movement (e.g. Elevating the bar from the floor while deadlifting).*

You're probably wondering, why three chances at cueing the movement? Well, the simple answer is because if it's taking you more than three attempts to put someone in the right position, you've made a mistake, you've chosen the wrong movement for that person at that time. And that's ok, you just have to fix it. Here's why.

First and foremost, and most obvious, if they continue to do the exercise while starting from a poor starting position, there's a real solid chance that something bad is going to happen. Not like step on a crack and break your momma's back type stuff. But the cumulative, misappropriated stress could end up causing an injury.

Second, and slightly aftermost, you're likely to make the client think it's their fault that they can't get the movement. It's not. They are in the wrong position...and that's always our fault as their coaches. The often, unfortunate outcome is a high level of unnecessary frustration. Sure, people learn at the point of struggle, this is absolutely true. But if you introduce them to a struggle that they aren't ready for, the struggle won't teach them anything other than inadequacy. You get three cracks, if there's no positive change, change the position.

Moving on from position, let's tackle movement and how verbal cues apply.

In most instances, movement implies a performance environment. That means we are using succinct, external cues—drawing attention away from the body and allowing the person to just move. Staying with the deadlift example, let's talk about moving from the starting position to the lockout position and a simple cue that helps clients coordinate their hip and knee action.

"Drive the floor away."

(A lot of times, if it's during the movement, I'll just say "drive." Just saying that, after the client has had a bit of time to understand context, implies that they should drive their feet through the floor to stand up tall.)

Driving the feet into the floor by "driving the floor away" is something easy to visualize and actually feel, making the cue a dynamic dynamo of deadlift performance. Everyone knows what it feels like to push their feet into the floor, and when we use "drive" as a performance cue we don't burden them with a bunch of unnecessary words or get them thinking too much about their body. It's nice.

Simple, external cues such as this are the tried and true sherpas of movement in a performance environment—if you've done the work up front to teach and build context (e.g. With positional cues such as macho man, sad dog, and tall and tight), they guide people to solid performance without a lot of conscious thought. Let your folks be sherpa'd by simple words rather than thinking themselves into poor performance.

In a learning environment, internal cues are sometimes appropriate to build context. Since the goal isn't performance, and we likely need to draw attention to something for people to gain awareness, sometimes drawing attention to a body part is necessary to create a point of reference. The cat-cow example from earlier is a perfect illustration. The client is moving, but we're cueing them to move their spine while saying spine so that they understand that it's their spine that is moving. Spine. We want them to integrate that into their movement understanding so when we move forward, or back, into deadlifting they can perceive spine vs hips without a lot of conscious thought. Understanding gained through context-appropriate internal cues seems to improve application of external cues in performance environments because folks have a more integrated understanding of their body in space. Then the analogies, metaphors, and action statements of external cueing hit harder.

Maybe the problem isn't positional or movement-based—maybe the lady or gent just isn't getting the movement, or they aren't focused intently on what they are asking their body to do.

If someone isn't understanding the movement that you're trying to teach them, well, it's your fault, not theirs. Understanding is all about building bridges between someone's currently held knowledge and the new knowledge they need to gain to be successful in a given situation. When it comes to coaching language, context is often built by understanding a person's experiences and using them to draw a connection between their life and the exercise you're asking them to do. Here's an example.

Chris Merritt and I work with a full-time, tactical, federal, law enforcement unit. Most of the guys are former military, have been to war, been through all sorts of serious mental and physical tests, and have spent a fair amount of time working with firearms. So, to help bridge the gap between the gym and their work, we often use firearms analogies. Chris and I each have enough firearms experience to create useful analogies, and the guys can easily understand the relationships that we create between operating firearms and performance training.

Examples like this illustrate why it's so important to get to know and understand the individuals that you're training. When you see them in the full scope of their lives, bridges to understanding are more easily built.

Understanding is also derived from physical ability. If a person is having a hard time with a movement that you're asking them to do, they just might not have the physical capability to do it—yet. In that case, all the verbal cueing in the world won't bolster their ability to demonstrate the movement. Intellectually, they'll likely be able to grasp it, but they'll not be able to connect the dots between their brain and their body. You'll have to change position.

Here's another note of importance: situations like the one described in the previous paragraph are why it's so important to do a movement screen with all of your clients before you start training them. Learning about their movement capacities and inadequacies as early as possible allows you to put them into positions that they can physically understand and demonstrate earlier in the process. It alleviates a lot of frustration on their part and wasted words, and likely frustration, too, on your part. And it allows them to move from "yet" to "able" in a much faster, more seamless process.

Focus is another multi-headed beast. There are more reasons that someone could be unfocused than there are Baby Boomers named Bob. And there are approximately 9 billion Baby Boomers named Bob (not a real statistic).

If it's a focus issue, as you might have guessed, your normal exercise cueing likely won't work as intended. Maybe it will—maybe the person just needed to hear a word that would snap them in. But, most likely, something else is affecting their ability to focus and they either need help putting that thing aside or they need some kind of pattern interrupt that brings them into the present.

Sometimes, breaking their cognitive pattern and helping them focus is as simple as making a statement like, "You don't seem very focused right now. What's up? Everything ok?" That might be enough for them to compartmentalize whatever is distracting them and allow them to get back to work. Other times, they'll tell you what's up and you can help redirect them by getting them to change their focus to exercise performance. This shouldn't devolve into a counseling session if there's a big issue going on. It's simply an opportunity to help them focus in on what they're doing by helping them to redirect their attention.

It helps a ton to make focus the first priority for folks when they walk through the gym door. The GAB system that we use to set daily goals, and focus in, is something that's helped our clients immensely to stay in the present moment of their training session. We'll talk more about GAB in the section on Aims and Goals.

For now, remember that being verbose is no good for no one. But using a well-chosen verbal cue that matches the environment and solves the actual problem, whether it's positional, movement, understanding, or focus, is often effective.

Let's move on to visual cues.

## *Visual Cues*

Let's start with a statement—visual cues sound a lot fancier than they really are, kind of like caviar. You get wooed by the name, but then you realize you're just eating salty fish eggs. Truly, visual cues are demonstrations of what to do and what not to do...as well as giving the client something to aim their eyes at. But don't let my downplay of the fancy name dissuade you, visual cues are super important and often necessary for a client's success with an exercise.

We use visual cues the same way in learning and performance environments. When teaching a new exercise, we always start with a solid demonstration of what to do before asking the client to perform the exercise. As we demonstrate, we introduce the coinciding verbal cues. Then we stand back, watch and let the client take a crack at the exercise without correcting them. It's part of our "let the first rep suck" philosophy. Letting folks try, and maybe fail, creates a great environment for teaching and learning. First, it allows them to learn the difference between poor performance and solid performance. Feeling what bad feels like before immediately being corrected allows the person some context about positions or movements they should avoid.

After feeling what bad feels like, we can demonstrate it for them, making our best approximation of what they were doing, so that they can connect their feeling with an image—taking full advantage of our sweet multi-sensory human experience. Two levels of understanding laid right on the ol' brain!

"Letting the first rep suck" also communicates that it's ok for them to try and fail—which is hugely important for their ultimate success. Learning is a process of exploration, and learning is at the foundation of any transformation. If we snuff out someone's eagerness to explore, or even baser than that, their safe feelings of exploration, by immediately showing them how wrong they are as soon as they try something, well, then we've completely undermined everything we are supposed to do as their coach.

Once we've established what bad looks like, we can again demonstrate what good looks like. Here's the flow:

Show them the exercise with a solid demonstration backed up by the corresponding verbal cues. Then, let them take a crack at the exercise. If they nail it, awesome! Let them know. If not, let them complete a rep or so without jumping in with a correction. Then, ask them to take a break for a second so you can show them what's happening—this is when you'll demonstrate what they're doing to so they can slap a visual on top of what they're feeling. After that, you'll demonstrate the correct performance again, so they have a contrast. I've heard my friends at Mike Boyle Strength and Conditioning call this visual cueing sandwich, "This, Not This, This." I really like that phrasing.

The "This, Not This, This," visual sandwich also works well for the first introduction of the movement. Start with a solid demonstration of the movement, then demonstrate a common mistake you want them to avoid, and then finish with another solid demonstration. After feeding them that sandwich, you can cut them loose to try the movement. Then, if they make a mistake, you simply return to the process above.

Now, what was all of that "giving clients something to aim their eyes at" mumbo jumbo? It's most easily illustrated with, but doesn't only apply, to medicine ball throws. It's simply giving them a target to hit. Many times, if you have a person try to hit a target that's at an appropriate height or distance it helps them move their body through the ranges of motion it should move through—without a lot of thinking on their part or coaching on yours.

For example, having a person throw a ball at specific point on the wall often does wonders for putting their body in a good position to move—the trajectory requires certain joint positions and movements. If they aim their eyes at a given spot, and they move to throw the ball in a way that allows them to hit that spot, they've been visually cued and reinforced by the satisfaction of achieving that very short-term goal. It's nice.

Eye aiming also works for aligning the body in a good position. Let's say that you have a lady or gent performing a squat or deadlift and you need to help them keep their neck, along with the rest of their body, in a good position. We'll just call that position "neutral." Having them aim their eyes at a point across the room—the distance varies so you'll have to pick one in the moment—and keep their eyes there as they squat, or deadlift, will help maintain that sweet, sweet neck alignment.

The important thing to keep in mind is that we are super visual beings and our eyes can often override our other senses—we need to take advantage of that. Whether it's through demonstrations of what to do and what not to do, or giving your client a target to aim at, visual cues are an imperative part of the coaching process. Give people the opportunity to process information visually and integrate it dynamically into their movement. Back it up with the rest of your cueing.

## Kinesthetic Cues

Sometimes folks just need a physical reference point to understand where their body is in space, where parts of it are in relation to other parts, and how to use all of that information to move. Touch, whether from another human being or from an object, is a lasting cue that also helps folks to quickly learn, and demonstrate, a new or improved movement.

I mostly use three types of kinesthetic cues in my coaching, and these are the names that I use for them, so if you know them under other names, I'm sorry, but this is my book. So, we're using my words! O'doyle Rules! Ok, so I use hands-on cues, object-reference cues, and reactive neuromuscular training (RNT) cues. We'll have a chat about each of them.

Hands-on cues are just as they sound, I literally put my hands on the client to help them find the best position possible or to help them navigate the movement. Wait, tap the breaks. You probably already thought of this, but it's good to ask permission before touching someone. There are, of course, relationships that carry-on over a long time and the permission is somewhat implied, but it never hurts to revisit that permission. And, before we go any further into this foray on hands-on cueing, make sure you check the laws in your state. Not every state allows personal trainers to physically touch clients, so make sure you're aware. And if you're not allowed, and you do it anyway, don't you dare blame me. (You: The guy in the book said I could, officer! Officer Handcuffs: Tell it to the judge, sister!)

There are four types of hands-on cues that I use every day in my coaching—*positioning, resisting, point of reference, and RNT*.

Positioning goes down during the set-up of an exercise or between reps. Think of all those times when a client's set-up goes awry, and your verbal cueing isn't getting the job done…and you physically guide them into position. That's hands-on positioning. I could carry on describing positioning, but I think the gist comes across better with an illustration.

Picture a lady or gent doing a set of incline dumbbell bench press, but as they perform the reps they have their elbows set too wide and they aren't pressing the dumbbells back far enough—ending with the dumbbells too far out over their chest and away from their shoulder joints. They're getting away with this mishap because the weight is kind of light, but if they continue on this way as they use more weight something bad is going to happen.

Knowing that words are only going to cause confusion at this point, you mosey on over and ask if you can guide their next few reps. They, of course, give you the affirmative. Then you carefully grab their closed hands and turn them to align their elbows at an angle around forty-five degrees to their body. After that, you guide them through a proper pressing path. With a firm grip on their wrists, you assist them from the top position into a good bottom position and then guide their press through a motion that takes the dumbbells back to the appropriate top position—somewhere in the vicinity of a spot at arms-length but above their face. You do this for a couple, or a few reps, then you cut the person loose to try it on their own. It sticks. Hooray!

The same works for set-up. If someone is doing a side-lying thoracic rotation drill, but they can't seem to get their legs in the right position, you help them out by moving them to the best position possible. Someone's back stuck in a super-flexed position before they're about to rip a deadlift off of the floor? Have them pause, press firmly but gently on the most flexed part of their spine, and ask them to "follow your hand" into the required tall and tight position.

Positioning is a great way for someone to feel their body moving from bad to good without the intellectual weight of words getting in the way. Sometimes just having another person physically guide us makes moving easier to understand.

Resisting, point of reference, and RNT are all weaved closely together in the tapestry of hands-on cues, so we'll talk about all of them at the same time.

RNT is the most complex of the three, so let's bang out a quick definition. During RNT, a dysfunctional movement pattern is driven further into the dysfunction that it's displaying so that the body's self-correcting mechanisms overcome the undesired movement. For example, a client is learning to squat with their bodyweight and their knee keeps caving in, so you press on the outside of that sucker and voila! The lateral muscle of the hip say, "No, no, no! That won't do at all!" and they start to do their job again—stabilizing the femur so that the knee doesn't cave.

Resisting and point of reference are subdivisions of RNT. While using a resisting technique, you apply some pressure on a segment of a client's body so that they feel something to push into. But it doesn't necessarily drive the person further into a dysfunction for self-correction like traditional RNT does. Let me explain with an illustration.

You have a lady or gent performing a set of rack pulls but they keep "scooping" their knees under the bar rather than driving through the floor and extending their hips and knees simultaneously. Verbal cues just aren't sinking in, so you walk on up to them and place your hand firmly between their shoulder blades and tell them to "stand up into my hand." Since your hand, and your pressure, is directly above the spot where they should be displacing force into the ground, the resistance teaches them where to push. Learning where to push allows them to "drive the floor away" and extend through the hips and knees simultaneously.

Essentially, you just gave the person a point of reference to move with, but the added resistance of your pressure changes the definition slightly. When using a point of reference, you're simply giving the person a little touch to either help them figure out where their body is in space or a subtle point to move around. Here are two examples.

A client is doing some sort of side-lying thoracic rotation drill with their legs stacked on top of each other. But as they rotate, rather than only moving through their upper-back and rib cage, their top leg slides on their bottom leg and their top hip rotates toward the floor behind them. No bueno. You, being aware of the no bueno-ness, drop on down to the floor and apply a little pressure through the top hip as you help them stack their hips back up. You maintain that pressure and ask them to perform a few more reps—your pressure keeps their legs and hips from sliding on each other. As you hold, you ask them if they feel the difference and if they think they could maintain that position on their own. Then you cut them loose to try.

Point of reference is also useful during the cat-cow exercise if a person can't sort out how to segmentally move their spine. Slight pressure on an individual vertebrae, with concise verbal instructions like "push into my finger, or arch away from my finger," helps folks figure just where in the hell that piece of their spine is. They now have a point of reference and they can integrate that point into the gross pattern. It's seriously cool to watch it work.

Now that we've hammered out all of the hands-on kinesthetic cues, let's move on to object-reference cues—which are similar to hands-on point of reference, but they use an object rather than a hand.

Ever align a PVC pipe, or some other kind of straight piece o' pole, aligned along someone's spine to teach them to hip hinge? If you just silently answered yes to yourself, then you've used a reference cue. Reference cues are simply using external objects to give clients an idea of where their body is in space and in relation to itself. Another common example is using a stability ball to help people maintain a solid arm to leg relationship during dead bugs.

The possibilities for reference cues are limited only by your imagination and, well, the things that you have lying around. Choosing when and how to use them is almost as expansive, but there are some simple parameters to help you decide when to use them.

Most of the time reference cues are appropriately applied in a learning environment that borders on a performance environment, and with a person that's lacking some situational, or gross, bodily awareness. The object is a better choice than a hands-on point of reference cue because they are going to use the object to perform entire sets. It would be kind of ridiculous, as well as impractical, to use a hands-on point of reference cue for an entire set. That's not so for an object-reference cue. They can appropriately give a person kinesthetic feedback for multiple sets, multiple exercises, hell, even multiple training sessions until the necessary awareness is earned and learned.

If you really need a position, and an accompanying movement, to sink in over the course of time, object-reference cues are dynamite-gold. I was going to choose either dynamite or gold as an obnoxious adjective, but I thought, why not up the ante? Use object-reference cues with your folks that really need a lot of input over a period of time to understand what a position, and a movement, should successfully feel like.

The doozy, the granddaddy, the pinnacle of all kinesthetic cues is RNT. We talked briefly earlier on about how RNT drives a movement further into dysfunction so that the body can self-correct and clean up a movement—and there are a ton of ways to use RNT. Let's break down knowing when it's an appropriate choice and a few solid examples for you to build on.

Like object-reference cues, RNT is helpful when improving movement over multiple reps, multiple sets, or multiple workouts. There are times, however, that it works as a quick movement reminder and then is removed. Either way, RNT is a powerful educator because it plays on two great natural functions of human movement: *we learn by making mistakes and we have a natural propensity to resist*. RNT amplifies the mistake and brings it to our awareness, and well, nobody likes to be "pushed." Also, like object-reference, RNT is appropriate with persistent positioning and movement issues. The differences being that object-reference doesn't necessarily feed someone further into dysfunction and that RNT is more appropriately applied in a loaded performance environment.

I bet you're wondering what kind of tools are appropriate for RNT. The most common tool is the elastic training band—jump stretch type bands and those small, flat broad suckers that are thin and super stretchy. You know the ones. But the reality is there are lots of great RNT tools. From medicine balls to chains, anything that you can use to safely nudge a person's movement and give them something to resist. Let's walk through some illustrations.

Here's one we've all experienced that's as guaranteed to happen as a morning poop after that first cup of coffee—a client sliding immediately into "Macho Man" posture (extension) as soon as they set up in a plank. Many times, it's a simple lack of lumbar awareness that causes this nearly inevitable movement malady. Other times it's a lack of capacity that causes them to lose their solid position and slide into an easier position maintain. Other times still it's because they've trained themselves to use a poor strategy. RNT can help to solve each problem—gaining awareness, building capacity, and replacing a poor strategy. And there's one simple application that works—lay something moderately heavy and flexible across their lumbar spine and have them hold that plank.

A chain, or several chains, works well.

The weight of the chain drives the back further into extension, into the dysfunction, raising awareness and giving the person something to resist against and correct their own movement.

How about those times when a person lacks lateral hip control during single leg movements and their knees collapse in? What a great RNT opportunity! Not only will the act of pulling the knee toward the midline of the body raise awareness and give the person tension to resist against, but it will also help to strengthen the lateral hip. Bang. For. Buck.

Anchor a band to the upright of something—a squat rack usually the most available option—and then have the person loop the band around their leg farthest from the squat rack, with the band running perpendicular to their body. The band should be pulling medially on the knee. Once you have the person set up, have them perform split squats and maintain control and alignment of their femur as they descend and ascend. Then, as they gain control and demonstrate more strength and proficiency, have them try some reverse lunging with that same RNT.

It's important to note that the tension of the band, or the level of any RNT input, should be enough to give the person feedback on position and tension worth resisting, but the person should be able to overcome it and maintain a good position for the duration of a set or series of sets. If they can't, it's too much tension.

Outwardly, it seems counterintuitive to push someone further toward the dysfunction that they are having, but trust me, RNT is one of the best movement education tools that a fitness coach can maintain in their toolbox. Keep the few notes on application from above in mind and then let the movement problems that you have to solve bring out your creativity. You'll have your clients moving impressively and you'll look like some kind of exercise wizard.

Now, that we've moved through RNT, let's put kinesthetic cueing to bed and move on. I'll keep saying that it's tough to completely segment out different types of coaching cues in a real-life coaching situation, but I'll also say that kinesthetic cues are often the most valuable that you can apply. People need to feel and integrate, and kinesthetic cues are truly the best cues for giving clients a feeling that they can understand and apply for themselves going forward.

Ok, on to environmental cues.

## *Environmental Cues*

Human movement is literally purposed by the environment. Our brain has our body respond to an environment, manipulate an environment, or simply move through an environment to achieve some kind of goal. It's, like, literally why we have a brain. So, setting up an environment for our clients that simply teaches them how to move without any excess talking, touching, or thinking is super cool and super productive. Environmental cues are also another type of tool that will make you look like Einstein's bastard great-grandchild—taking all that genius and applying it to exercise.

Environmental cues are exactly what they sound like—using the environment, or making small changes to the environment, to teach or correct a movement. They're used to improve position and movement path, making them dead ringer in learning and performance environments. And the best thing about them is that they are instant teachers—they offer immediate feedback about what went right or wrong with a rep.

Why do environmental offer such great and immediate feedback? Because we set them up to do so. We are controlling or creating an environment for the sake of educating without speaking—for the sake of letting a client's body educate itself. I can understand if that sounds ambiguous to you, so we're going to walk through some environmental cues.

Here's the scenario: your client is doing kettlebell swings and every time they hike the bell they swing it too low between their legs rather than hiking it up into their hips. The result is a discombobulated swing and a lot of spinal flexion. Not good.

You give the client verbal and visual cues—you could talk and move until you're blue in the face, but nothing is sinking in. So, here's what you do…you stick something between the client's feet that forces them to hike the bell up into their hips. If they don't hike high, they're going to smack that thing (at our gym we use medicine balls…we have some sizable ones).

During the first rep with your newly utilized environmental cue in place your client smacks the hell out of it and realizes that they are hiking too low. It clicks! Hooray! The next rep is a little higher, they just brush the top of the object. Then, Eureka! They hike the bell perfectly and snap up into a beautiful swing.

Smacking the implement between their feet with the bell instantly educated them and gave them an obvious, negative outcome to avoid. The result is an instant association between how they were moving—the position of their body and the path the bell followed—and the negative outcome. "I don't want to do that again!" They think to themselves. With that instant feedback in mind, they make a small movement improvement. (Let's take a minute to bask in the corniness of that last sentence.) After that, there's one more small improvement, but they still make a small error. Ok, they can note that. Then, finally, they move flawlessly and nothing bad happens. There's an instant reward, and our old pal dopamine helps them remember what they did to totally avoid the bad thing. It's pretty cool.

We don't always have to manipulate the environment to create a cue, often times we can use it as is. The floor, the wall, the squat rack—all of these immovable structures that give shape to the space around us serve as powerful movement educators. Let's walk through a half-kneeling example.

You're teaching a client the half-kneeing position (one knee up, one knee down) and they have a super hard time keeping their up leg in a good position with their hip, knee, ankle, and foot all in-line. Instead, their knee is diving in and, consequently, it throws off the alignment of the rest of the joints from the lower-body all the way up through the spine and into the shoulders. Everything you've learned about their movement capabilities lends you to believe that they can handle the position, they just need some awareness. So, you make a quick, environmental change.

Moving from the open floor, you set the client up so that they are in front of a post of a squat rack—the medial shin and knee of their up leg is aligned adjacently to the post and only an inch away. The goal is to keep their leg from touching the post—it automatically trains them to keep their knee from caving in. The rest of their body follows suit and they find solid alignment. It's very nice.

## Closing Out Cueing

I don't typically like to just tell people what to do—it probably stems from my own aversion to such leadership—but I'm about to make a strong recommendation that leans not so subtly toward telling you what to do. There, fair warning. If there's only one thing you remember from this discussion on cueing, make sure it's that cueing isn't just a verbal phenomenon.

Remember that cueing makes use of the rich human sensory experience to help folks learn, understand, and consistently produce movements. Our job with cueing
is to match the sensory experience to the person and

to the circumstance—and given our ability to understand environment, personality, visual inputs, kinesthetic inputs, and auditory inputs, we have no excuse not to take a real-good crack at individualizing our cueing.

We have one more paradigm discussion left. Let's talk about what we do when a client demonstrates successful movement.

## Dramatically Reinforce Positive Change

There's a self-perception problem that pervasively intrudes our human, psychic reality: we too often view ourselves as cold, rational, logical, and decision-making beings like Dr. Spock, when in reality we're irrational and emotional beings much closer to emulating a high-functioning pleasure-seeking monkey. (We're apes, not monkeys, but you get the gist.)

Sure, this is a spectrum—some folks are more rational and less emotional than others. But we're all irrational and emotional at some level. Each of us also wants to be seen and acknowledged. It's basic humanity. Dramatic reinforcement during our coaching helps us plug in to all of this humanity to foster clients' progress, imprinting lessons in our clients' memories so that they can replicate the movements we're teaching them.

Below, in no particular order, are dramatic reinforcement strategies that work. Here's the deal—just like the cues we discussed, dramatic reinforcement strategies are tools in a coaching toolbox, you pick the right one for the right job. Keep that idea present in your mind as you read on.

## Match, Plus One

Just as we do while using all other coaching tools, we begin with a consideration of the individual. Dramatic reinforcement is a matter of the client's perception. What one person perceives as a positive, fun experience is far too outlandish for other folks. Then there's
that whole vice versa thing. Keep this in mind—meeting folks at their level helps ensure that our dramatic reinforcement is perceived positively. Quieter folks need less rah-rah, extreme extroverts need some noise and palpable excitement. So, we meet people at their level, and then go one notch above to make the interaction an event.

To limit abstraction and make this applicable we use an excitement scale from 1-10—1 being the least excitable and 10 being the most. For example, say you're working with one of your less-excitable clients, she comes in at a 3 on the excitement scale most of the time. To reinforce her dramatically, you come in at a 4 after she does something successful. That way she has a positive interaction, feels seen, feels dramatic reinforcement, without being overwhelmed with too much sis-boom-bah!

The same process works for your folks higher up the scale. Have someone that lives at a 6? Reinforce them at a 7.

Do this in your own way. If you're not a crazy and outlandishly-expressive person, don't feign that you are one. But in your own manner, within the confines of your own personality, find a way to match your clients' levels and then go one above to make the event dramatic.

Simply consider the individual. What words will impact them? Does appropriate physical contact resonate with them? Is your tone fitting for the celebration and the person?

### Celebrate Small Victories, They Accumulate

Consistency and momentum are the most impactful change drivers. Unfortunately, they are often dismissed by coaches and clients while folks seek the grandiosity of huge, unrealistic, one-time events or changes. And many times, we mistakenly reinforce this misplaced behavior by celebrating the big and visible without acknowledging all the small steps that actually created what we see.

To foster consistency and momentum, we need to celebrate the daily, small hurdles our folks are jumping. Don't be mistaken, we have to keep celebrating the milestones, that's super important.

But we must make the little things dramatically important so that demonstrable transformation is possible. We have to reinforce the behind the scenes work.

This is simple work. Comment on effort, congratulate folks on consistency, and celebrate small improvements in technique. By celebrating the seemingly mundane and unimportant aspects of training we help folks accumulate, compound, and create the goal-achieving changes our people work for.

When we do celebrate the big hurdles, we celebrate them appropriately.

### The Best Thing That Happened Today/The PR Board/What Has This Done for You

On the wall, adjacent to the entrance at BSP NOVA, is a rectangle, chalkboard-paint table called *The Best Thing That Happened Today* board. At the end of each shift, morning and afternoon, the coaches recount the last few hours in search of the great things that happened. After a chat, or a quick think if the coach closing the shift is alone, the most noteworthy and positive thing that happened during the shift is written on the board.

On the wall directly in front of the strength training area is the PR board. It's also a chalkboard paint rectangle, and every time a member sets a PR during the month they write their name, and the milestone reached, on the board.

In front of the consultation office there's one more chalkboard paint rectangle. This one asks clients, *What has training at BSP done for you?* On this board folks write up things they've done in their everyday lives that they wouldn't have achieved without training. Some folks list that they've been overcoming poor health markers due to chronic autoimmune disease. Others tell silly stories about sprinting from terminal to terminal to catch a flight. (When you think about it, it really isn't all that silly. It's seriously helpful life stuff.)

All of these boards dramatically reinforce positive change. On the *Best Thing That Happened* board clients are acknowledged for their achievements by their coaches. The other two boards allow the clients to ring their own victory bell and shout, "Good for me!"

Combine all three and you have an environment full of visual representations of change brought about by positive action. Dramatic reminders that reinforce all of the effort expended toward worthy outcomes.

You don't have to run out and paint your walls in chalkboard paint and let people write on them. But it's not a bad idea. Reality is you just need ways besides talking to let people know they're kicking ass. If you can find a way to make that resonate throughout your environment, do that. This is true for all fitness coaching environments—from one-on-one in commercial gyms to boutique-style group training.

You could send out cards.

You could send follow-up emails after people do rad shit.

You could use a private Facebook group to celebrate successes together.

There are millions of options. You know the ones that suit you, your people, and your environment. Choose them and do something with them.

**Continually, Dramatically, Reinforce**

Be cognizant of who's in front of you and give them an experience that they'd perceive as positive and affirming. Continually celebrate the little steps that take us from point A to point B. Celebrate the big moments appropriately, by making it seem appropriately big. You'll connect with people humanly, emotionally. You'll help them remember what they're doing right. You'll help them remember why they chose to train with you.

## Teaching and The Paradigm in Closing

Direct, on the floor, coaching is where we do most of our work as fitness coaches—putting structure to that work is absolutely paramount to our sanity and success. And for our clients to experience the same S words. We need consistent, simple ways to give people information about their movement so that they can incrementally improve it. Or, if skill takes a temporary lapse, they can regain it. People also want to know that they are on the right track and that they are being seen taking steps on that track. Direct coaching by using this paradigm, or a similar one, meets our clients at a human level, helps them connect with the information that we're trying to give them, and demonstrates that they are seen and heard.

Open the door to coaching with bright spots while also avoiding hammer and nail fixer syndrome. Be sure you know what you're looking at, and then communicate that information succinctly. When you cue, make sure it matches the context of the environment and the person. And, by God, when someone improves let them know that it got noticed.

## Guidance in Closing

We are guides. It's that simple. The main priority of our professional existence is help people navigate the land between their Point A to the closest approximation of their Point B. While there is simplicity in understanding our main role as a fitness coach, there's a bit more complexity in carrying the role out in the real world. But if you have consistent processes to follow, like understanding that we provide structure, we help with accountability, and we teach, and you follow them consistently, it makes the seemingly confusing elements of guidance much simpler.

It begins and ends, however, with remembering that we *are* the guide and not the hero. When we accept that fact we can give our clients the space to take ownership of their training and improve our work at creating the environment that allows them to do so. Here are the main things I want to leave you with after this chapter.

I want you to remember that you're the guide, not the hero. Yes, I know started every paragraph in this conclusion with a not so subtle reference of that fact, but it's that important. Remember that a consistent structure for helping folks that encompasses everything from helping them set goals to using appropriate cues is absolutely imperative. It all needs to fit and be cohesive, but it doesn't all have to happen overnight. Use your own coaching principles and build the scaffolding in pieces. And make sure you have a consistent process for delivering your coaching on the floor.

Our Paradigm is a great example that's worked for a number of years now. Feel free to start there and expand outwardly. But I'll prod you to develop something of your own, something that *you* actually own. I'm not saying this because I'm worried about my intellectual property. I'm saying it because when you work to create something on your own, using elements of what you've learned from others, you better understand it. Then, when it breaks, or something doesn't work as planned, which will inevitably happen, you'll know how to retrace your steps and fix it.

Above all, remember that you're the guide.

# Pillar III: Aims and Goals

During the course of my career I've noticed something curious about goal-setting—a lot of folks feel like they should be able to do it, and they try, but they truly have no idea how to set a goal and act towards it. They try and either come up with a goal that sounds nice but isn't true to themselves, or they try and fail because they just don't have a process. And others still avoid goal setting all together because of the lack of knowledge that I just mentioned or because goal setting denotes commitment—and fear of failure is as real as the computer I'm typing these words on. This common goal-setting knowledge gap de-motivates folks and banishes their worthy goal ideas to a deep abyss shrouded by talks of "maybe next year."

What people often fail to realize is that goal setting is a skill that needs developing, not just something we're supposed to be good at. It's like learning to squat or deadlift. It's like learning to drive a car. Goal-setting is a skill that is composed of different sub-skills that allow folks to connect with what they want, see themselves in a future state of attainment, and then act to close the gap be between themselves now and that future self they envision.

Keeping skill development in mind, we approach goal setting with our clients using a process that begins with simple skills and then grows in complexity over time—most of that complexity coming from being able to project farther and farther into the future. And as we build these skills, we give them tools to develop themselves as goal-setters. With writing prompts on the back of programs, handouts that help them decide what they truly want to currently act on, and conversations, we guide our clients into becoming goal-setters.

We begin with the smallest unit of time that we can handle, the training session. Starting so small gives us two advantages—it allows for frequency, folks have to think about, and work on, the goal-setting skill every day in the early going. And it works with a unit of time and level of specificity that isn't too abstract for folks to grasp before they have a solid goal-setting skill set. It's simply getting in the reps and setting clients up for concrete success in a time-frame they can manage. We'll talk about it in the section on GAB.

As clients finish their first program, we start working on longer time-frames. We set goals for their next phase of training, which in BSP NOVA land translates to mean the next four to six weeks. It's a nice next step. In consideration of the future, four to six weeks is totally intellectually manageable—it's not that hard to project oneself forward a month in time. Also, everything
that's necessary to achieve the goal is actionable in the program. The client can envision, plan, and see

the product of their envisioning and planning directly reflected in their program. Then they can almost immediately act. Phase-long goal-setting is a great intermediary step between the extreme laser focus of GAB. Sessions and the farther off world created during long-term goal setting. We'll talk more about it in our section on progressing from program to program.

When a client finishes four programs at BSP NOVA it's said that they've finished a block of training. This takes anywhere from four to six months depending on how many days per week the person trains with us. During the course of finishing a block, a client has had a lot of opportunities to GAB, and they've had four, phase goal-setting chats. Translation—they've been getting the reps to build their goal-setting skills. At the very least, they are in the habit of projecting themselves forward—even if only poorly. Poor skill is a step forward from no skill.

Our End of Block Meeting is a thirty to forty-five-minute conversation that reviews the last four months, helps the client figure out where they currently are in their training and transformation process (this brought on the invention of the "Where Am I At Wheel" hold tight for that), and plans the next four blocks of training in levels. A perfect planning world has the levels build on each other to achieve a bigger end. In this process, each program breaks down as a level, helping the client to take the more abstract, long-term, bigger-scarier goal and break it down into actionable and achievable chunks that allow them to demonstrate, and feel, their forward movement. We apply the same process to year-long planning, with the blocks breaking down as bigger levels and programs remaining as parsed, practical chunks. Our chat on this process comes in the section on coaching longer-term goals.

I've saved the last description for our most recently evolved goal-setting tool—the *Where Am I At? Wheel*. Along with noticing that folks have a hard time setting goals, I've also noticed that they often have a hard time taking complete stock of their current situation. They have a hard time taking the 30,000 foot view of where they currently are and analyzing what they're doing well, what they aren't doing so well, and what they could potentially act on to move themselves forward. Really, they're just not sure where they're at—and it can produce a lot of frustration. If someone isn't totally sure where they currently are, it's difficult to accurately project into the future with action that's relevant to making progress. We knew we needed to do better with helping people sort that out for themselves...so the *Where Am I At? Wheel* was born, and we added it to our End of Block meetings. The *Wheel* gets its own section, which is coming right up by the way, but we'll talk about it in our section on coaching longer-term goals as well.

Our process for goal-setting momentum continues on for the duration of a client's life as a member at our gym. The GAB process doesn't go away just because someone gets a little farther down the path, we continue to help folks set their daily focus. End of Phase chats drive the immediate direction, and potential redirection, of what folks aim to act on and accomplish during the course of a program. And once we've reached the stage of longer-term projection, that continues on. Ok, let's start breaking this stuff down starting with the *Where Am I At? Wheel*.

## The Where Am I At? Wheel

One of our coaching values at BSP NOVA is to "be the GPS." Throughout each session, and over the long-term, we help our clients figure out where they currently are in relation to where they want to go. It's a balance of short-term, and long-term, direction and re-direction. A chosen course of action goes well until it doesn't anymore, then the coach and the client as a team, re-calculate to navigate past the obstructions. Thinking of ourselves as the GPS has helped us home in on our day-to-day coaching actions and client communication. But we noticed something that caused us to update our operating system—clients weren't totally clear on where they were starting from, and it was holding them back from choosing the courses of action that precisely aligned with what they wanted to accomplish. They didn't, in the scope of the holistic transformation process, have a good enough picture of where they currently were.

Don't get me wrong, they were taking action, making positive changes, and we were guiding them through the process with some useful tools. But we knew we could do better—we knew that we could get more specific with regards to each person and their individual level of need in all of the different areas that promote transformation. And it started with me sitting at a lecture.

My buddy Jon and I went to see Dr. Jordan Peterson speak at the Warner Theatre in D.C. As Dr. Peterson paced across the stage, weaving together a conversation on interrelated topics, I did what I always do when listening to someone speak or reading a book—I thought of the information within the context of the problems I was currently trying to solve. Then the Eureka-moment happened!

Dr. Peterson was speaking about depression and how he counsels folks that come to him for therapy. Essentially, he and the person do an examination of the person's life in regards of the things we typically value in Western culture. Does the person have a job? How about a fulfilling romantic relationship? Are there any friends? Is there an avocation or hobby? What are things like with the family? I'm pulling this from memory, so there are likely one or two that I'm missing. But, essentially, these questions attempt to help the person find the answer to a bigger question—*where am I right now and what do I need to know to be sure of that?*

That's the question that smacked me upside the head. It put our clients' issues of figuring out where they are in their transformational journey, and how to act on where they are, into perfectly visible context. We needed our own series of questions that answered that question—*where am I right now and what do I need to know to be sure of that?*, but instead of helping folks battle depression, we were helping them take greater ownership over their training and transformation. We were helping them be better aware of current, actionable strengths and weaknesses.

I left the theatre with my mind racing, immediately formulating notes in my head about creating a tool that would help our clients determine "where they were at." But I also knew that for this tool to be as effective as it could be, I couldn't build it on my own—so I took my idea to our staff meeting and presented to the BSP NOVA coaches. After walking them through the spiel that I just laid out above, I asked them what they thought the characteristic actions of our most successful clients were. In which areas of their lives did they consistently take positive action that ultimately helped them to transform—and maintain that transformation?

To provide context, we thought of specific clients, their actions and their results. The result was this list:

- Commitment to something purposeful
- Consistent training
- Connection and support
- Activity outside the gym/fun
- Active self-care

- Creates mental space

- Sleep

- Nutrition

Chris, the handsome devil that he is, happened to be away during this momentous staff meeting, so I laid this all on him when he was back in town the following week. He, of course, loved it, but he had a killer upgrade to make—he wanted to give clients a visual that immediately illustrated their current level of balance, their current strengths and weaknesses. His idea was to create a wheel.

We pretty much immediately sat down and started playing with Microsoft Word and Excel, creating a table of points that would illustrate a wheel in real time. As the person was rating themselves on the wheel the coach would fill in a data point in a table and that would immediately construct an image that reflected back the client's level of balance—as well as their current strengths and weaknesses. If they're performing exceedingly well in one area, but not managing to make any headway in another, it's immediately apparent. Their wheel is filled out and round on one side and flat on another. Or maybe it doesn't even look like a wheel, but a series of jagged disproportions that demonstrate a person's glaring inconsistency of action. No matter the situation, they're immediately made aware.

The best thing about the awareness the person gains is that it isn't through some abstract list of numbers that are tough to place. Sure, the person is a five in this area, but what does that really mean to them? An image, often times, is a superior expression of meaning. People can extract what an image means for them in context. The rating allows for the creation of the image, and the relationship between the two gives the person concrete understanding.

We needed ratings criteria to bring the Wheel to life and make it actionable. So, I took the list of characteristics, sat with them for a week, and reviewed past client successes even further while also combining that with my common training and transformation knowledge. The result was two to four definable actions that clients could examine, within the realities of their own lives, to give themselves a rating in each area. Don't gloss over the fact that the client self-rates. We'll talk more about that in just a bit, but it's purposeful and important, so make a mental note to check in with that. Here's what the ratings criteria look like:

Once we had the Wheel program set-up, Chris trained me in on how to enter the data points, and we had the criteria, it was time to launch this puppy. We reasoned that the most fitting place for the Wheel was during our End of Block meetings. If folks have reached the End of Block point it means that they have at least some momentum going, they have at least a general idea of where they are headed, and they have context enough to evaluate themselves and their progress based on the ratings criteria. The Wheel could now help them illuminate their strong and weak points during the past four programs. I started putting that Bad Larry in play in two different ways.

Luckily, I had two End of Block meetings almost immediately after we finished the Wheel. They were the perfect opportunities to try it out using different strategies. During the first meeting, I introduced the Wheel right away—using it to frame everything else we'd discuss in the meeting.

## The First Roll of the Wheel

As I sat down with the first client, a fellow named Gerald (not his real name), I explained that we've been working on a new tool to help clients get a better handle on where they currently are at in their training journey—that it'll explore their current strengths and weaknesses to give them a clearer vision of how to plan the actions that will take them to the next level. Then I asked if he'd be in to give it a go—and wouldn't ya know it—he said yes!

I handed Gerald the criteria sheet and explained that all of the different points on the wheel, and the criteria used for self-ratings, were based on what our most successful clients have done to transform physically, and in the mental and emotional realms, during their time at BSP NOVA. (Here's the cool thing, Gerald was one of the example people we used while constructing the Wheel criteria! The plot thickens.) Then I let him know that he'd be self-rating, that I was available as a resource to consult and that I'd ask him some open-ended questions if he needed help clarifying things for himself, but that I wouldn't be rating him. Then we got to work giving shape to Gerald's Wheel.

Here's what good, old Gerald's Wheel looked like after his self-eval.

We learned that Gerald had true drive to accomplish something important to him, that he felt connected to and supported by people inside and outside the gym, and that his rigorous sports schedules kept him active and having fun outside of the gym. Conversely, we also learned that Gerald was neglecting to take good enough care of himself. It was something that he had a vague consciousness of but not a total awareness that empowered him to act. That changed.

Gerald came to the meeting with a partially-filled-out End of Block form (you'll learn more about those in the section on "Coaching Longer-Term Goals") but had not totally prioritized his action steps toward the transformation that he wanted to actualize. The dude was, and still is, excited about strength training—he'd already made an incredible transformation in a short amount of time, losing around forty pounds in under a year. Learning new things and getting stronger intrinsically drives him—he's one of those dream clients. But he layered on top of that a desire to "feel athletic again" and to "feel as good as he did when he was starting a baseball season in high school."

Here's the thing, high school wasn't just last year for Gerald—at the time of this writing he's in his mid-thirties. Any of you that have entered your thirties, or moved beyond, know that it's impossible to get away with the same silly shit that younger folks strut about doing. *Those young folk* can eat like absolute derelicts, add alcohol as a staple fuel source in their diets, and pretending a nap from 3 AM and 7 AM constitutes a good night's sleep, still perform. Of course, they shouldn't do all this Tom Foolery, but they can and can get away with it. If we folk a bit farther down life's path behave that way, we end up with week-long hangovers, oppressive diarrhea, and energy levels that make zombies look spunky. Again, this info wasn't anything totally new to Gerald, but he wasn't totally aware of it. Lack of awareness and strategy put him in a transformational holding pattern.

Now that we had awareness, we brought in his End of Block form and had a look at where he wanted to go over his next four programs. Mostly he was focused on developing strength and movement skill—the intent was to improve his depth of knowledge and also develop strength and mobility. But his baseball and softball playing escapades were a caveat to all of that.

Gerald was playing four to five adult league softball games per week and about two adult league baseball games per week. The dude loves smacking dingers and rounding the bags—who am I to tell him not to? We needed to formulate a plan that fit with his summer and fall plan of playing a lot of ball and being able to develop his body.

The outcomes, and levels to achieve them, that he outlined on his End of Block form gave us direction for programming, but it didn't address his Wheel, which was obviously flat on the bodily maintenance and recovery side. So, using Gerald's newfound awareness, we had a deeper look at nutrition, sleep, active self-care, and creating mental space.

Our conversation continued with some simple action-step framing—what's the low-hanging fruit, what's the big "frog" that you could eat first, and what are you actually ready and willing to do right now? Some folks like the challenge of eating the frog first, which means doing the most difficult, displeasing thing. Most others, however, choose to grab that low-hanging apple and munch that sucker, get some sweet satisfaction, and then use that to build momentum forward. I don't know that either approach is better, or that one is more "right" than the other—it's individually dependent. That's why I ask.

Gerald leaned toward the low-hanging fruit option, but he did acknowledge that he'd like to do something to move forward and change his current situation (more on this in our second story). Then we had a look at the Wheel and talked about what he was ready and willing to address at the time. Nutrition, rated in the middle-ground at three, he reasoned, was where he'd like to start. He'd already built some momentum during his time at BSP NOVA with making better food choices based on the basic education he'd received, and that felt good to him. He had some previous momentum to build on. Besides all that, he just wasn't in the place to address the other lagging areas. And that was totally ok.

Our nutrition dialogue truly only encompassed two things (two things that most everyone loves, I might add)—good food and alcohol. Although he'd been consistently making better food choices, Gerald still leveled that he was eating out too much and wasn't taking enough responsibility and control over his own nutrition. He also acknowledged that he was drinking more than he should be—more nights of the week than not and more than just a drink or two. It was a social thing that accompanied playing baseball and softball. These answers popped forth out of Gerald because I asked what he thought his current biggest struggles/things he'd like to work on with his nutrition were. Then we got super honest about being ready and willing.

I asked if I could share a thought with him, and when he granted me permission, I said something to the effect of, "Cutting back on the drinking is probably going to have the biggest impact on improving your nutrition, but that has to be something you're truly willing to do. Are you there right now?" He responded with a polite, but sincere, no. The drinking and social aspect of his softball and baseball life was important to him and he wasn't ready to make any kind of change associated with it. So, we looked elsewhere. Knowing that his situation with alcohol wasn't going to change, Gerald decided to attack his nutritional consistency with something simple—keeping good food in his house. It took a little conversation and few steps to get to that decision.

We started off with a general question, "What are a few other things that you think you could do right now to improve your nutritional consistency?" Honestly, I don't remember all of the list items, and we wrote those suckers on the whiteboard, so their specifics are lost to the ages, but I'll hit you with the gist. The main point was that Gerald wanted to "take the power back" (thank you Rage Against the Machine) and be, at least a little more, in control of his nutrition, and stop eating out so damn much. We worked together to narrow it down to a specific action item from a list of potential action items by considering the ultimate outcome and what he saw feasibly working with his life as it currently flowed.

How'd we narrow it? We used a technique that I learned from Coach Steve from Habitry during Mark Fisher Fitness' Motivate and Move lab. The process is called 5/3/First. Using that general question from above as the Idea Inception Generator (something I just made up), we listed out potential action items. I don't remember if we hit a total of five, but we had enough good options to start narrowing down. Once we had those options out on the table, actually the whiteboard, I asked another question. "Ok, so out of all of these, which ones, let's say three, are you most ready and willing to do right now?" And then the list was narrowed. We continued on in the same fashion.

"Alright, so of the three we have now, which one do you think you're most ready and willing to start with?" Gerald chose consistently buying groceries—I'd give you the rest of the list, but I don't remember the other items. We had a place to start! Hooray! Now we had to talk about how those groceries were consistently going to be purchased.

There are a lot of resources out there on helping people make change, and many of them guide coaches to help clients make change as seamless and easy as possible—especially in the early going. The resources say this for a profoundly simple reason—it works. With that in mind, I asked Gerald a question, "What's something positive that you're already doing that you could piggy back your grocery shopping onto?" I let him sit with the question and I kept my mouth shut. After a bit of a pause, he had an answer.

"Well, I consistently train on Wednesdays, I think it would be easy to just grocery shop every Wednesday after I finish training. I'm already out of the house, I feel good from training, and I could just stop on my way home," Gerald replied to my question.

"Feel pretty confident you could get that done? Ball park it, scale from 1-10, 1 meaning not at all confident and 10 meaning absolutely certain," I followed up.

"I'd say a 9. I know I'd like to do this and just attaching it to my gym sessions will make it easy to get done," Gerald asserted his confidence. After that I recapped the plan, and we chatted about potential obstacles and strategies to overcome those obstacles.

"So, we're going to start with grocery shopping every Wednesday after your training session and you feel confident that you'll be able to get it done because of the ease of attaching it to your training session and your desire to do it. Word. Is there anything that could potentially get in the way and stop you from grocery shopping on Wednesdays after your sessions?" I asked.

"I mean I guess missing a session on Wednesday could be an issue. And I'm sure there will be times that I just don't feel like doing it," Gerald replied with some consideration.

"Ok, cool. What do you think you could do about each of those things?" I threw an open-ended question back at him.

"Well, if I miss Wednesday, I'll just attach it another one of my sessions throughout the week. Not feeling like going is a little trickier. I guess I'll just keep my goals in mind and how much I want to be able to perform while playing baseball and softball while also developing my body," Gerald strategized in return.

After that, we did the Predator, bulging biceps, hand-clap greeting.

The Wheel gave Gerald awareness of where he was currently at. We used that awareness to set priorities, help him decide what he was ready and willing to do, and choose a single action that he could incorporate into his life to embody his priorities. That's pretty cool. What's even cooler is that at the time of this writing
it's been about six months since Gerald declared that he'd grocery shop and he's still doing it. He's even maintained the habit by swinging by the grocery store for some sushi even if he doesn't need groceries just to make sure he keeps the Wednesday-grocery store-habit going.

### The Wheel's Second Roll

Penelope is a lovely woman currently in her mid-30s. She came to us after years of exercising on her own while also dealing with a lot of associated trials and tribulations. To protect her anonymity, we won't go into the details of her trails, but know she's walked a hard road. During the time leading up to her first roll of the Wheel, my second time rolling it, she had made a ton of progress with her training mindset and she was ready to project herself a bit farther into the future, rather than working with only a month or so at a time.

Here's the thing—Penelope didn't like planning, but she happened to be much better at it than she thought she was. But not enjoying planning, and thinking she was bad at it, held her back from exploring all that it could be for her—at least up to this point. Knowing that about her, I thought it could be helpful if we got the conversation rolling first and used dialogue to build momentum before rolling the Wheel. Using the Wheel up front might kill the conversational mojo with her, so I let things get rolling and let her get some of her thoughts out—then I used those thoughts to guide her to the Wheel. My logic was this: she needed some conversational momentum and some ideas to consider about her future before slapping the Wheel down in front of her. That way, the planning has started, and the Wheel was simply there to direct, or re-direct, as a GPS as needed. In another apt analogy, we weren't going to turn the GPS on until we started to get into an unfamiliar neighborhood.

Like I said, Penelope is much better at planning than she gives herself credit for. She usually has a clear idea of what she wants from her training, what it's going to do for her on all levels of her life, but she doesn't like writing it out and articulating the steps. It's more discomfort and uncertainty than anything else. Deep down I believe she knows she can do it, but thinking of it in action steps just isn't her jam—fear of failure rears its ugly head. With this in mind, we never truly got into an unfamiliar neighborhood during the meeting we are currently documenting, although she did get a little stuck. But we worked out that stuckness with simple conversation and got all of her action steps articulated and on to paper.

So, there we were, a vision crafted and action steps clear and on paper—no apparent use for the Wheel, so I thought. In the name of experimentation, however, I asked Penelope if she'd like to try out a new awareness tool we developed just to see if it gave her any other insight. Being the congenial soul that she is, she complied.

We rolled the Wheel, walking through all of the criteria, me helping with open-ended questions that subjectively fit her situation so that she could apply the criteria to herself, her thinking critically and explaining where she thought she currently was, and self-rating based on that critical thought. The outcome was an accurate snapshot of Penelope's current training life—she was able to think, describe, and rate herself with an astute self-awareness.

"Is there anything on here that you'd like to address or is it just cool to see it for awareness of where you're at right now?" I asked as we each took stock of her

Wheel. She replied that she wasn't ready or willing to address any of the areas of the Wheel, that it was just nice to see where she was in relation to all of those areas.

And there, dear friends, is the second great use for the Wheel beyond using it to plan action steps on weak or strong areas. Awareness, tracking, and demonstrations of progress is just as powerful as using the Wheel to plan. Penelope wasn't ready to do anything with that information, it was good enough for her to see some of her lagging areas and where she was strong. There were other actions to take not directly related to the outcome of the Wheel, and that's where her readiness and willingness lay. That's great. I didn't prod or try to persuade her to address the Wheel, I left it be. The Wheel was for her to use for decision making, not for me to use to over-coach someone.

With that awareness in her back pocket, Penelope went off to act on her plan and she made significant process toward her goals during the course of a training block. Recently, at the time of this writing, she had another End of Block meeting with me. We laid out one of the final stages toward her ultimate goal and we checked back in on the Wheel, updating her ratings as I filled in the numbers in the spreadsheet to show the changes in real time. And, well, things had changed.

The shape of the Wheel morphed to fit the changes she'd made in her life. Some things remained constant, others improved, others declined slightly. And she was happy with the progress and the visual. For the second time, she was happy just to see the changes and didn't want to consciously, and directly, address anything specifically that she learned from the Wheel. It had served its purpose for her and she already had the direction she wanted from completing her End of Block form—direction was established, and awareness gained.

I don't think the importance of the discussion in the last paragraph can be over-stated, so I'm going to expand on the themes just a wee bit more. It would be easy, and likely the default action, to prod someone to act directly on the information they gained from their Wheel. It's like walking into an orchard full of sweet, succulent peaches, seeing all the low-hanging fruit and the person accompanying you saying, "I just don't want anything sweet right now." And you're like, "What do you mean? Look at all these fruits! There are beautiful fruits everywhere just for us!" But if someone doesn't want any fruit, they don't want any fruit. We can't make them eat the fruit.

The Wheel isn't a weapon that we wield to assert our coaching dominance and push our clients toward fixing something, it's a tool of awareness that allows clients to get think critically about where they currently are in their transformation process and see a visual representation of their current place. If they're ready and willing to act on that awareness, great. If not, that's totally up to them. This principle extends beyond the Wheel and into the rest of our guidance, but this seemed like an appropriate time to drive that point home.

## The Wheel Keeps Rolling

As I mentioned during our discussion on Penelope's rolls of the Wheel, it's not a static document. It's a living, evolving picture that gets updated with each End of Block—visibly demonstrating the change, or lack thereof, that a client has made over the period of time between meetings. Giving people the opportunity to compare themselves across time is illuminating for them. It can either give them the opportunity to celebrate their growth or help them take in the emotional weight of not changing in the way that they'd like to. It could be the necessary prod to begin making the positive change that they desire.

For this to happen, the Wheel has to keep rolling, the client has to continue to see the changes to their Wheel over time. A one-shot look is great for an awareness of their current place, but long-term, sustainable transformation needs not only a path to walk, it also needs a little history to drive decision making about where to take the next step on the path.

## Why Self-Ratings?

To some folks, the answer to the question of this subtitle is obvious. But obviousness doesn't imply detailed understanding, it just implies a seemingly "duh" like sensation when we read or see something. Sometimes that feeling of obviousness makes us believe we know more than we do. To use a little hillbilly slang, that dog won't hunt. So, I think a detailed explanation of *"Why self-ratings?"* is in order. When you understand the decision, you'll be better able to make a similarly productive one for yourself.

**Unconditional Positive Regard**

Carl Rogers, that phenomenological maestro, projects his voice back into the conversation again. Let's assume that we value unconditional positive regard, that it's foundational to our coaching philosophy and practice. This is definitely true for us at Strength Faction and Beyond Strength Performance NOVA, but I'm bringing you in on this, so you have to roll with me. In agreeing with that, we have to do the best job we can to maintain an environment based on that regard. Making direct judgments about what a client is, or isn't, doing is a great way to mess it all up.

The damage to unconditional regard isn't necessarily on our end as coaches, we can evaluate how someone is doing in a given area and still separate that from our regard for them as human beings. A potential problem arises from the client's perception of the relationship. If we make the ratings it can appear as though we are sitting in judgement of how they are handling themselves and their lives. That could lead to them feeling as though our regard for them is contingent upon their positive or negative actions. The further, and overtly insidious, potential outcome is that they act in a way that they think is in accord with what we want and not necessarily what they value or see as true for themselves. We don't want this.

Introjected values, values adopted from others rather than being self-generated, are much harder to live by because they may not be totally in line with what a person truly values and/or wants. They also guide people to believe that they must live up to some external standard set by their coach in order to make progress or even deem themselves worth approval. The latter is an extreme case, but I've seen it happen and it isn't pretty. It's best to avoid it.

At some level we all introject ideas and values—it's part of how society gets along. But in the fitness coaching context—which is very personal and should be guided by a client's actual wants, needs, and values—introjected values have no place in helping a client determine the training path they should take. An alignment of general values, which usually helps a person decide whether or not they're going to train with you, is another thing altogether. And it's a good thing. Introjection, however, has no place.

This is not all to say that we can't share our opinions with our clients—sometimes it's helpful and at times it might be necessary. However, in a context where our opinions can be interpreted as a direct judgment, it's best to leave them be. The Wheel, and any similar tool that you may develop, is a place to leave our opinions be.

**We Aren't with Them All of the Time**

There's insight into our clients' lives that we just don't have. Sure, we can use the information that they give us to generate a rating, but, in that instance, we are only getting a surface level interpretation of the story. Also, if we create an environment in which clients feel as though they can fully tell us the truth it's more likely that they will and that we'll have accurate information to consider. While that may be enough to make an accurate rating, we still aren't in their heads to see everything that's going on when they are living out different aspects of their lives. They are.

Even though humans are complex, and we for sure do not have a total understanding of our individual choices and behaviors, we still are actually with ourselves in all of the situations we live out. No one else is. We may not have a total grasp on why or how we did something, but we usually know what we actually did and at least a foggy grasp of the context surround that action. So, while we see patterns of behavior across clients, and we can likely induce or deduce reasoning and apply a rating, we aren't the best source to make the rating. The client is. They are living the decisions and the actions.

That's not to say that we can't provide general commentary on what we've observed during their time with us without ascribing a valence to any of their actions—that could be useful in helping them consider their own situation. We're usually best served by practicing the OARS (open-ended questions, affirmations, reflections, summaries) techniques from motivational interviewing to help them come to their own self-commentary.

**It's Their Process**

That's really it. It's not our process, it's theirs and they need to take ownership of it. A self-evaluation empowers greater feelings of ownership in the process than a rating from an external source like a coach—self-validation reigns supreme. The goal is always to help clients internalize processes so that they may gain self-awareness and progress toward a level of autonomous mastery. Considering their own current standing based on successful patterns exhibited by people like them (the Wheel Criteria) within the context of their own desired outcomes and values, and what they can choose to do about that standing, promotes internalization of skills and thought processes that lead toward autonomous mastery. It's the end game, and it's our job to help them move toward it.

## Recapping the Wheel

The Wheel is a creation that grew out of necessity, teamwork, and the successful actions of clients that transformed. It's become a source of awareness that helps clients determine where they are in relation to where they want to be and what direct actions could take them closer to their transformational ideal. In case you want to build your own kind of Wheel or awareness tool, let's have a look at the components that make this sucker up.

*First,* there was an idea, the inception of which coming from a known lack. We didn't have a good enough tool for helping our clients sort out exactly where they were in their training and transformation process. The idea was illuminated by harvesting information from another context—a psychologist talking about treating people with depression—and figuring out how to apply it in our setting.

*Then,* there was the consideration of the patterns of success we'd seen over the years, and in what areas success seemed to matter for our clients. Read: what actually helped people positively transform. As a team, we used examples drawn from the actions of living, breathing people—not some nice ideas from a text book—and created a list of qualities that were observably demonstrated by clients that took themselves to a better place.

*After,* I thought about criteria, based on the same kind of observations that gave us the qualities, that would allow a person to rate their current status on each quality. This generated two to four criterion for each quality that our clients could apply to themselves, in their own living context, and make an honest appraisal of how they were currently doing.

*Next,* we sorted out a combined program, using Microsoft Word and Excel, to generate an image that clients could see in real time as they made their ratings. Seeing the shape of their Wheel, be it totally balanced
or flat on one side, gives them a more concrete understanding of where they currently are rather than just the total abstraction of seeing numbers on a page.

*Finally,* we put it to work, and it's been working ever since. The first two clients that tried it during their End of Block meetings—Gerald and Penelope—allowed me to play with a couple of different ways to present the Wheel. Now, the process of applying, learning, and updating continues. I've seen clients experience "A-ha!" moments and I've seen some figure out better courses of transformational action for themselves. Even better, now that more clients are seeing their Wheels updated after a training block or two, they are gaining perspective on how different seasons of their life affect their training and lifestyle goals. And they're able to note their progress, or lack thereof, as they analyze their current and past behaviors within the context of what they're aiming for.

It might seem odd that I snuck the description of this tool, something we use mostly during our longer-term planning meetings, into the beginning of this chapter. But, just because we use it that way doesn't mean that you have to…maybe it would be a good initial consultation tool for you (we've actually considered using it during our initial consultations). Plus, I wanted to you have an understanding before we get to the section on our longer-term planning meetings—we call them End of Block Meetings—so that you'd know just what in the great blue blazes I'm talking about.

Now that we've got the Wheel rolling, let's back up to the shortest-term goal-setting tool we use on the daily with our clients. They're called GAB sessions.

## How to GAB

People often have a hard time managing what's not currently plopped in their laps—and even sometimes, well, a lot of times, even managing those things in their laps is difficult for people. We need simple structures that help us guide our actions toward progress. Without them, it's hard to make the requisite sacrifices, and to enact strategies and actions that take a human being from the current point to a future, more desirable point. Hell, without them it's tough to know whether or not we just did something worthwhile.

Goal setting structures, no matter the time frame associated with the goal, give us the chance to denote something meaningful and then act in a way that coincides with achieving that meaningful thing—that meaningful thing could be a better emotional state, a skill, or an event like deadlifting 500 pounds before you get married.

People need other people, armed with a good structure and the ability to ask questions, to help them plop that meaningful thing into their own lap—and those plops need to be different sizes. Some plops cover years, and some months. Other plops are weeks. But we also need plops as short as an hour or so—effectively the time that most training sessions get slated for. Help people direct their intent for an hour and you'll help them build the skill to direct it for longer periods of time.

GAB is the best tool we've found to help a person plop the next hour of their life into their own lap and ask themselves what they're going to do with it.

## GAB Where's It Come From?

GAB stands for Goals, Assessment, Barriers, it's borrowed from *Motivational Interviewing in Nutrition and Fitness*. Their use, however, is a little different. As we use it to set an intent for a training session, they use it to get people thinking about their goals at the end of a nutrition counseling session so that they can make successful progress between sessions. It's a great progress-building bridge between contacts, and we've used it that way at the gym and with Strength Faction, but I love it most as a tool for focusing and setting a direction during a training session. (P.S. If you haven't read *Motivational Interviewing in Nutrition and Fitness yet, get on that.*)

## So, What's all this GABing Do?

Let's start big picture (goal-setting skill building) and work to smaller focus (what it gives us for the task at hand) in answering this question.

GAB starts the process of thinking through what it takes to achieve a goal, while building the skill and practice of setting, and achieving, goals in an ultra-manageable time frame—which subsequently builds the necessary skills to set longer-term goals. It gives folks the chance to say, "I want this to happen before I leave the gym today" and gain some momentum-building success with goal-setting. People need to feel competent with smaller tasks before they can successfully move on to bigger ones—and feel as though they can actually order their actions in a way that achieves the bigger task or outcome. GAB is the small task that preps folks for the bigger task of setting, acting towards, and achieving a longer-term goal.

It also gets people thinking about what they'll need to achieve goals. GAB gives them the answers to questions like:

- *What do I want?*
- *Do I truly believe I can do it?*
- *What resources do I need to get what I want?*
- *What do I do when things don't go as planned?*

Answering these questions about a short time frame like an hour can build the competence and confidence to answer these questions over, and about, longer periods of time. It can do wonderful and wondrous things for a person that has a hard time articulating what they want and what they're going to do about getting it.

In the short-term, within the context of the training session, it gives clients a focus and a way to direct their actions toward that focus over the course of the session. The process gives them something to aim for, as well as a chance to prioritize their actions and think through how they'd overcome any obstructions that block them achieving their aim.

It does a fair bit of good for us coaches, too. It tells us exactly what we have to focus our coaching on for the day—especially when someone gives us their perceived obstacles toward achieving their GAB goal. That's where they see trouble coming, and that's where we can best guide them through bushes, killing tigers on the way, because that's where they want to be guided. They tell us, even if indirectly, where they want to be coached.

### How Do We GAB?

*Here's a quick preface: this might seem stiff and sterile at the beginning, but it becomes more natural and conversational with practice.*

It starts off with a client and a coach examining the program together. The coach asks the client what they'd like to focus on or achieve during that training session. The program is the path, and GAB tells us all how we're going to walk down it for the day.

## The Goal

So, we look at the program and ask what they'd like to do today. A lot of times folks will say something like, "I'm not sure." That's where your coaching and observation skills come in. If you know there's a particular exercise, or a bigger goal, that's important to the person, have a look at the program with that context and start asking the person questions in reference to that exercise or goal. If you know that the person likes bench pressing, but doesn't have a well-articulated long-term goal yet, chat with them about bench pressing. They may want to focus on that for the day, they may not. But it will at least get them thinking.

If you know someone has a longer-term goal, say improving a race time or something similar, ask them what, if anything, they've been struggling with in their training right now or if there's something in particular that they'd like to accelerate with their training that the day's session could help with.

These forms of questioning will pull some kind of aim out. And, here's the thing, when you get something, even if it seems like some feeble, little, insignificant thing, go with it—especially if goal-setting is new to the person. If someone has some reps under their belt, and you're sure they can do better, hold them to a standard by continuing your questioning. Again, consider all of this within the global understanding you have of the person's personality, desires, and current place in their training process.

**The Assessment**

Once we help them mine a daily aim out of themselves, we get a confidence integer. That's the A in GAB. We ask them, on a scale from one to ten, how confident they are that they can achieve the aim—one being the least confident and ten feeling like their confidence is going to burst right out of their chest.

They'll pick a number and we'll ask them why they didn't pick a lower number. The questioning goes a little something like this, "Awesome, so you're an eight with that goal today. That's pretty confident. I'm sure you have some good reasons. I'm just curious, why did you pick eight and not seven?"

This gives them a chance to evaluate why they feel so confident and further talk themselves into being able to do it. After they give their reasons, ask them if their confidence is still at the same level or if it's gone up. A lot of times people will talk themselves into a higher rating.

If they give an answer of seven or lower, however, it's probably best to move on to another goal for the day. Continue to scan their program, and any previously-stated longer-term goals, to find a focus for the day that they feel confident in approaching.

**The Barriers**

"Ok, so you chose a solid eight, but you didn't choose nine or ten, so I'm assuming you see something that might get in the way of you achieving that today. What might that be?"

That's the question that typically leads us into the discussion on potential barriers.

This question launches them into an expedition through the jungles of gym circumstance to find any potential tigers that could swipe them on their way to a successful training session. Once the tigers are found, we can kill them. There's always something that could get in the way—there's always a tiger. Always. People will often say that they don't see anything that could…that's when you need to ask another question or two to get them to think more deeply about it.

Sometimes, if the daily goal is small enough, or you're totally sure that it won't be a problem, let the person to ride high on their confidence and kick ass. But it is a rare occasion that nothing, absolutely, nothing could get in the way of achieving the goal for the day. It doesn't mean that you have to poke and prod and be a doomsayer. But you do have to say that you're pumped that they feel so confident, and you want them to keep that confidence throughout the session. And the easiest way to do that is to make sure that they have a strategy for any potential problem that could come up. Then, with both of you thinking with more focus, ask again.

## When to GAB

GAB, in this context, is best done at the beginning of a training day as the client is examining the work that is planned for the session. It's also good to GAB at least once per week with a person so they start to build skills they can internalize from GABing. The ultimate goal is to get them to internalize the GAB conversation so that they can start to have it with themselves. The goal is to make them autonomous in their direction setting.

## A Bit o' GABing

Let's check out an example of a GAB conversation. The coach and the client are looking over the program and all of the training slotted for the day.

*Coach:* Alright, Debbie, what would you like to get done today? Is there anything in particular that you'd like to focus on?

*Debbie:* Well, I'm not sure. Just have fun and not get hurt I guess! (Debbie finishes with a laugh.)

*Coach:* Alright, well, that's a good start! Do you think there's something more specific? You have hex bar deadlift and dumbbell chest press on the docket today. Either of those feel like something you'd like to focus on? What about any of the exercises that you're doing today in relation to your goals?

*Debbie:* Will deadlifting make my butt bigger? I'm working on that right now!

*Coach:* It certainly can!

*Debbie:* Ok, let's focus on that today.

*Coach:* Cool! So, what would you like to focus on with deadlfting today?

*Debbie:* Well, last week I just felt like I wasn't doing something right...like I didn't have my back in the right position or something. It didn't hurt or anything, I just didn't feel like I was doing it right.

*Coach:* Ok, so you want to focus on your form today?

*Debbie:* Yeah, I'd like to make sure my back is in a good position.

*Coach:* Cool, so if you had to put a number on it, one to ten, how confident do you feel that you can figure out that back position today?

*Debbie:* Oh sheesh, I'm not sure. I guess I don't think I was that far off last week, something just didn't feel right. I don't know. I guess an eight or so.

*Coach:* Alright, great. So, why did you pick eight and not seven?

*Debbie:* Well, I don't know. I guess I feel like I can figure it out and I'm pretty sure you can coach me to do it.

*Coach:* Cool, I like that. So, do you think there's anything that might get in the way of you improving your deadlift form today?

*Debbie:* I guess what kind of coaching I get. What I mean is sometimes I don't necessarily understand the words when I get told to do something, sometimes I need to see it and feel it. So, if I can see it and feel it I'll probably get it. But if you just talk to me I probably won't.

*Coach:* So, you want me to do some good demonstrations and use some other tools to help you feel the position?

*Debbie:* Yes, that would be great.

*Coach:* Ok, let's do it!

## G.A.B. And Your New-er-ish Clients

At our gym, GAB sessions take a paramount importance with new-er-ish clients. Remember all of that skill building talk from the beginning of this section? We want as many opportunities as possible to build goal-setting skills with our new-er-ish folks before they finish their first program and sit down with a coach for their first End of Phase chat. When they have that End of Phase chat, they'll need to be able to take stock of their wants, their needs, and the actions that will help them achieve both in a longer time frame. A bunch of exposures to planning, and acting, during shorter time frames preps them not only to gain an understanding of where they're at, what they like/dislike, and what they want, but it also gives them increased opportunity to build goal-setting and acting skills.

Most clients start out with us training two days per week in our small group personal training program. That's eight chances per month to GAB. That's eight opportunities for them to internalize a process of considering what they want, projecting themselves into the future, and acting.

## A GABing Recap

- GAB at the beginning of a session at least once per week with a person to help them internalize the process.

- Nail down a goal for the day. If it coincides with a longer-term goal, great. If not, that's ok. Just help them get something out.

- Use the assessment to help them figure out if they really want to do the thing and to help them talk themselves into a higher confidence rating.

- Be real about barriers. There's always something.

- Consider hammering it home even more with newe-er-ish clients

Let's move on to our End of Phase planning process. We use it to help clients guide their next month of training and to gain the information we need to effectively progress their training programs.

## End of Phase Chats: Progress from Program to Program

A client just finished a program. They've spent the past four to six weeks working hard, and there's been some good, as well as some bad. It's time to look forward to the next program...what do you do now? How do you coach the person to productively move forward while considering the necessary elements of their training program?

We have a process for that.

**First Thing's First!**

The first thing to consider is the perfect scenario—that the program goal is attached to a bigger, longer-term goal. Is there a block (four program) goal or a bigger year-long goal? If so, the first thing to consider is fitting the focus of the next program into the long-term plan while also evaluating where the client currently is.

But reality doesn't always manifest that perfect scenario. In fact, it's not typically the case. The goal should always be to develop a long-term aim to strive for. Continually setting our eyes on the horizon helps us to keep our feet plodding toward it. Part of that plodding, however, is getting better at setting goal—I know, broken record time again—and getting good at setting short-term goals will help us get good at setting long-term goals. So, if we can get people to focus in and articulate what they'd like to achieve over four to six weeks, that's a great step on the way to long-term goal planning.

**Here's What Goes Down...**

On the day that someone is going to finish their program, they walk into BSP NOVA and find their program on a clipboard and standing up against the window, rather than laying down on the windowsill. This gets them to pay attention to it and remind a coach that they need to have an End of Program Chat when they finish training for the day. The vertical clipboard is also a reminder for the coaches that a given client requires special attention that day.

Then they train. That takes a little while. Usually an hour. If it takes more, we put a foot in their ass. Not literally. Figuratively. And it's a gentle foot. More of a prod. Sometimes a foot though.

When the training is done, they plop their buttocks down and fill out the back of their program form. It looks like this:

We have them fill it out on their own, and do their own writing, for several reasons.

First, writing something out is like making a declaration—there's more emotion tied to it and it's also easier to remember and attach to. Second, we want people to write and think for themselves without our influence before having a discussion with them.

Then, once they've finished filling it out, they let us know when they're ready, and we swoop in to chat them up on what they've written. And when I say chat them up, I mean ask them open-ended questions and reflect what they say so that they can get further clarification on what they're trying to do. We have a sequence we follow during the chat. Let's have a look at it.

## What Just Happened?

We always start with the commentary about the program that they just finished. It helps with expectation management and sets the stage for the rest of the discussion. This is also a great opportunity to learn about how someone generally felt about their past program—that pertains to every detail, from the exercises they performed to whether or not the feel as though they've progressed.

Getting the good, the bad, and the ugly out lets them push their own process forward and it helps us get better at our jobs. This is where we really have to tune into our curiosity—especially if there's some bad and ugly written down.

When we read through this part, we ask questions about what they wrote. If they achieved their goals, and things went well, the question could go something like this.

*"So, you feel like you nailed this one! That's awesome. Why do you think things went so well?"*

And if they didn't feel so good about things, we might ask a question like this.

"So, I noticed that you don't feel like you achieved your goals and that you're on a back slide. What do you think happened?"

Then we build on those questions in either direction. We listen. We have conversations like human beings. We learn. We need this part of the conversation so that we know how to go forward. If there's a problem, we have to talk about it. If we don't face the problem, then we can't work together to fix it. If everything is going famously, we have to know what we can do to keep the momentum rolling.

Then we talk about moving forward.

**Goals for the next phase?**

Here's the thing, sometimes people need to talk a bit more to get everything sorted out. Other times people are all set with their eyes focused forward. We have to be ready for both scenarios. If someone needs to talk more to get what they want, and how they'll act to get it, in focus—the first indication is them struggling to write it down—then we need to ask some questions to help them think through it. But if someone has clear, declarative goals written down, and the associated whys, we leave them be.

As we ask open-ended questions, we keep the program, and what the client wrote, between us so we can both look at it as we talk. We aren't the keepers of the information, and we want the person to be able to reference what they wrote as they think. Also, as we ask questions, and get people to elaborate on what they meant or what they want, it's best if they write out more of what they were thinking.

Let's say we asked a few questions about a potential new goal that someone wrote out. Our questions got the person thinking, and they gained clarity on what they were trying to do and how they wanted to say it. In that case, we ask them to write down what they said—for the same reasons that we had them write in the first place.

Once the client and the coach are in a good place with everything, they slap hands as they bid each other adieu. The next time the client arrives, they will have a fresh new program that's entirely based on the conversation that they just had. That's pretty cool.

Here's what's even cooler—what they said is summarized and placed at the top of their next program. Their goals are listed there for them to see every time they come in to train. It gives them recurring reinforcement that they were heard and puts their goals in their face on a regular basis.

**How will we know it's working?**

Expectation management—that shit is important. People also need to see themselves making progress—

it matches expectation management in importance. They need to know that their struggles are being validated. Stating how they'll know it's working allows them to create that validation for themselves. It also gives us an opportunity to learn how they think we can best do our jobs to help them. Their expectations may be a little off kilter from reality, but at least answering this question gives us the chance to talk about it.

Having them state how they'll know it's working allows us to have a real conversation about expectations—especially within the context of timeframe. (More on that later.) It also helps us keep things in order. If someone says that they want to lose ten pounds, but they'll know they're program is working if they can deadlift ten more pounds, well, there's a mismatch. Believe me, this happens. Now, we have the opportunity to have a conversation about it rather than letting confused expectations catastrophically play themselves out.

### *Our Main Job In All of This*

Our role is facilitator. We are like a sounding board that a client uses to hear themselves as they craft their path forward—and we are also there to guide and advise along the way. To do that job, we use a few tools.

## Tools for Clarification

Our clarification tools are open-ended questions and summarized reflections. Most of the time, despite what we might what to believe, people do their best thinking as they are speaking. Thinking is a motor action, and the tongue carries out that action. Being able to talk to another person helps someone sort out what they are really thinking—or go deeper on what they are thinking. Open-ended questions, the ones that require more than a yes or no answer, allow people to talk and elaborate. And as we continue to ask questions based on their answers, people can think and elaborate more until they end up at a solid understanding of what they want to do and how they're going to do it.

Here are some examples of open-ended questions:

- *Tell me more about that (not really a question, but it works).*
- *Why do you think that is?*
- *What else could we do?*

Summarized reflections help in a similar way. When we reflect something back to someone, we do our best to summarize what they said and repeat it back to them. This allows them to hear what they said so they can be a little more objective about themselves. It also shows them that you're actively listening to them, which is not only good for rapport, it's also good for keeping them engaged in the conversation.

Starting off reflections with a statement like "If I'm hearing you correctly" and finishing with, "does that sound about right?" gives the person a chance to comment and keep the conversation rolling.

Sometimes reflecting someone's goal or "so that" statement back to them, without any lead in or finishing question, is enough to get them talking.

There's a balance to strike between open-ended questions and summarized reflections and there isn't an absolutely right or best way to find that balance. Just be a human being, be curious about the person that you're talking to, and stay in the conversation and good things will happen.

**Action Tools**

The biggest action tool we provide is the program. It is literally a structure for physical action. GAB is the second line of defense to help them take specific action. It takes the program and chunks it up into day-to-day wood chopping. Four to six weeks can pass quickly and without focus if we don't have a tool to bring our eyes to the day we have at hand.

There are also those things the clients decide they'd like to do during the time that they aren't with us at the gym. We help folks list them out and set up an accountability system so that they can stay consistent. If you can work these into your coaching, do it. People are with us for short periods of time. If we can help them manage the other hours of the week, they have a better chance of succeeding.

## What Can Happen in Four to Six Weeks?

This is important—what's realistic for the course of a program? Often, our folks don't really know, so we have to help them set realistic expectations. Many folks will undershoot what they can actually get done in a month or a little more. Keep this in mind as you have these conversations. If people need stretched a bit, don't be afraid to help them get a little uncomfortable. Other folks will need some real talk on what can actually happen in that amount of time. We have to be willing to have that conversation, too.

Either way we have to put people in the best position to be successful. Whether we let them undershoot or we patronize a ludicrously zealous short-term goal, we aren't doing the best that we can as coaches.

Frame your thoughts with this in mind.

## End of Program Coaching Recap

- Remember that your role is facilitator
- Have a sheet for them to fill out
- Let them write
- Ask open-ended questions and reflect answers
- Let them write again
- Stretch those that need it, reign in those that need it

A month is great and all, but it's only a smaller segment of time in the grand scheme of training and transformation. Sure, a lot can happen in a month... especially for a new-er-ish trainee. But creating a long-term vision and crafting a plan of action toward achieving it ultimately is best. We can work backwards. We can create more stability in action. And we can draw a mental image that helps incite excitement about commitment.

## End of Block Meetings: Coaching Longer-Term Goals

It's time to do some longer-term planning. A client has just finished a block of training—four training programs—or is looking to forecast out for a yearlong journey into the world of physical development. This is very cool. We like this.

Longer plans, however, require...well...more planning, as there are more necessary steps to completion. In the simplest terms—folks have to take more action, in more stages, to get the goal done. We have to consider looking ahead while also supporting every day action. There must be a vindication for the struggles, and we need something powerful to avoid as well as something rad to work toward. Within all of this we need tools for framing, tools for acting, and a solid position to guide someone from.

We'll chat about all of this using the End of Block meeting structure at BSP NOVA as our guide.

### *The End of Block Meeting*

Before we get rolling, a quick, two-part preface.

First—each End of Block meeting at BSP NOVA has a slightly different flavor. Sure, everyone fills out the same forms, but the content of each meeting is different depending on the individual. The structure essentially remains the same, but different tools might be necessary, at different times, during the course of the meeting. I'm going to present all of the possible tools we use, but just know that they don't all get used every time. It varies.

Second—the EoB structure is used for yearlong planning as well. The structure—the levels, etc.—just expands out to fill a year rather than four months. It's the same break down, only blocks become bigger levels, programs become levels within the blocks, and on down to daily action. This, sports fans, is a perfect world. We don't always get a perfect world. But, just know that the structure doesn't have to change to plan longer-term.

*Here's how it goes down:*

As a client is approaching the last week of their training block, the coaches notify me, and I email the client a link to our End of Block Meeting form. Once the client fills that out, we schedule a meeting in the form that they prefer—sit down, phone call, email.

They have the option to do a complete re-assessment, FMS and all, although this is rarely chosen. Most folks choose to just sit down with me in person, a smaller few choose to do a phone call—usually because their schedule doesn't match up with a sit down—and fewer still choose to just have an email exchange. Up to the time of this writing, I think there's actually on been one email-based End of Block meeting in the history of BSP NOVA. The take-home point is that we give them the option of choosing how they meet.

I email them the form ahead of time to give them time to think and write—at least a few days. Chances are they're going to have a hard time filling out the levels, and that's totally cool. That's why we're here, to help them sort it out and get clear. We're like a young Obi Wan Kenobi...without the light saber or the force.

I budget anywhere from thirty to forty-five minutes for these clarity-seeking meetings, and during the course of the meeting I use the EoB form (I print it out and bring it to the meeting) as a reference for each of us. I use it to ask open-ended questions and to reflect answers back to the client. They can peruse their writing and elaborate—and, if necessary, handwrite in more.

When they first sit down, I say something like, "Ok, catch me up and walk me through this," in reference to the EoB form. Then I sit, listen, and ask questions to understand and, when necessary, to help the client get clearer. As the fog lifts, I have the client state things in clearer terms and write down those more clearly stated things—be them goals, levels, etc. Since we mentioned goals and levels, let's talk more about that process.

Even with solid instructions, a form to guide them, and time to think, a lot of people have a hard time crafting block or yearlong goals and levels that march them into achieving those goals.

Goals by themselves are often scary to most people—the potential that exists within a goal, declaring it, stating a path to achieve it, and committing to that path is enough to cause a lifetime's worth of second guessing in a minuscule amount of time.

Sure, they could apply themselves and earn something awesome. But they could also fail—and that's a big tiger for people to slay and move past. Many times, the tiger manifests itself in statements like, "I don't know
if this is a stupid goal or not", or, "I don't know if any of this actually makes sense." Sometimes they are correct in wondering if it makes sense, but most of the time it's a pre-emptive cushion because they're judging themselves.

So, many times folks come in with only one or two levels filled in—sometimes without any. Other times they come in with levels that don't match with the goal they've declared.

*It's all evidence to reiterate that this is hard for our clients, and they need our patient guidance to direct themselves toward something they want.*

When folks are stuck, open-ended questions are a mighty savior. That stickiness often leads them to ask us what we think their levels should be. We have to do our absolute best to avoid telling them what we think the levels should be—even if it's obvious and staring us right in the face. I've found the best course of action, in this case, to respond with something like, "Honestly, those would be my levels, not yours. I think it would be better if you came up with them and I just helped you think through them, cool?" Then we redirect back into the conversation. They may prod a bit more, trying to get their levels stated for them, but it's absolutely necessary to hold fast and resist the prodding.

When the client gets stuck, it helps to start with the goal and start asking questions about it that get the client to elaborate. A "so that...", or why, statement is especially useful here. "I want to achieve X so that I'm able to do Y." If a person knows why they are doing something, it's easier for them to flush out a path to get to their goal. A lot of times this gets them to elaborate enough for the levels to become clear so that they can write them out. And as those levels come out, or get clearer, the client fills in the lines.

Here's an example.

One of our clients at BSP NOVA told us that he was planning on doing two weeks-worth of hiking in New Mexico and he wanted to be prepped for it *so that he could enjoy himself while he was on the trip*. With this in mind, we talked about his current training if it was enough to prep him for two weeks full of mountainous scenery walking.

He decided it wasn't.

So, I asked what he thought he needed to do to be prepared.

He said that he needed to maintain his strength while improving his cardio and doing more hikes on the weekends to prep for actually being out there. (No kidding, this came out of *him*. It wasn't my doing. Great stuff, right?)

Then we could take that statement and break it into four levels so that he could systematically step closer to the thousands of steps he'll take per day on his trip.

The levels went something like this:

1—Maintain strength training while upping gym cardio and adding in 2 hikes per month

2—Adding in more gym cardio while maintaining strength and going on 4 hikes per month

3—All the same while doing 8 hikes per month

4—All the same while increasing the intensity of the hikes

Once we had a clear goal, and a clear why, we could lay out the steps to get there. Now, parts of these goals/levels aren't super specific—that much is true.

"Maintain strength while upping gym cardio" is somewhat abstract and not totally time-keyed and measurable. But he knew what he meant by it, and it got him going in the right direction, so we went with it. As people continue to do this process, their goals get more and more specific. We have to take what's in front of us and work with it.

**What if they just can't figure it out?**

If a person is struggling to get out a longer-term goal and a level system to achieve it, we cut the time frame back and focus smaller. Sometimes it's right to stretch the person and challenge them to think through it. But sometimes we just have to stay within a timeframe where a client feels competent and play the long game by building the skill and prepping them to think longer-term next time. Maybe the person is having a hard time conceptualizing a full, four-program training block but they could manage to project two programs ahead. Go with two programs.

*The Other Tools*

What if someone's having a hard time getting specific or figuring where they want to start? What about the little action steps that will help them achieve each level? That's where 5/3/first comes in—a technique we learned from Steven Ledbetter.

The client lists out five potential things they could do to take action toward achieving their goal(s). Once they have a list of five, they narrow that list to three priorities. The three things are then narrowed to the one thing that they'd like to prioritize and start with. The other five things don't go away—and it's important to remind the client of that so that they don't feel like their options are being taken away from them. They are just starting with the thing/action that they chose because it's either the most important place to start or what they perceive as the best place to start. This works for building out levels, actions in between levels, daily habits, etc. When someone gets stuck and needs to list out ideas or has a hard time setting priorities, bust this technique out.

## *Heaven and Hell*

There are two powerful stimuli that motivate people to action—envisioning something they absolutely want to avoid and envisioning something that they strongly desire. Having both conditions clear in the mind's eye gives people cause to plot a course and act. If we articulate what we don't want, we can begin to act in a way that keeps us from ending up in that negative condition. And if we have a vision of what we desire, our steps away from what we're avoiding are even more productive. They're taking us toward something that we want.

The exercise we use to draw this out of folks is called Heaven and Hell and we adopted it from the Self-Authoring writing program. We mostly use this to help our clients when crafting their visions, but it's also a great tool for when people are stuck during an EoB meeting. Having to think, envision, and write seems to help people to set goals and chunk them into manageable actions and achievements. The writing allows people to tell themselves what they actually want. Then they can "mine" their vision for the goals and action steps to achieve it.

It's a simple process. Set a timer for somewhere between five and thirty minutes, depending on the length of time you're planning with the client, and have them write, unedited. Start with the Hell condition—have the person write out the absolute worst scenario they can imagine for themselves within the context of their training, health, nutrition, or whatever you're working on together. Have them describe what it looks like, what it feels like, and how much their life sucks because they didn't do the things they needed to do to avoid this pit of hell.

Once they've written out their hell, have them craft their heaven. The same timing rules apply, but this time they'll write out the absolute best thing they can imagine for themselves. What does it look like, what does it feel like, and how much better is their life because they took the positive actions they needed to so that they could achieve this vision?

This process can work even for folks that don't have a vague idea of what they want or want they want to avoid—if they're willing to let themselves write in an unedited, hot pen, stream of consciousness fashion. It's scary for some people and they'll block themselves from going deep enough to write the sincerest version of what they're thinking. But even writing a shallow approximation is helpful. It still helps the person to get clearer and gives them something to aim at. They don't need perfect aim, they just need to aim. If, however,
a lady or gent is willing to let themselves write at full depth, they can pull things out that they didn't even know where there. The completely opaque becomes clearer. And their initial vague representation of their future training life becomes something clearly actionable.

**The Perfect Breakdown**

What if everything works out perfectly? The client sets a goal for a year out and then develops the corresponding levels and actions between levels to get it down. What does that breakdown look like?

This:

***Yearlong Goal:*** Something slightly scary that makes people strive

- *Levels to Yearlong Goal:* 3 blocks of training (a block is 4-6 months)
    - Each block has a goal that corresponds with the yearlong goal
- *Training Levels in each block:* 4 phases of programming
    - Each training phase as a goal that corresponds with the block and the yearlong goal
- *Weekly Actions:* GAB focus for the week or day
    - This could also be a weekly "One Thing"

The person has a big thing to strive for, something that will take fifty-two weeks-worth of effort. That's laid out first.

Then we look backwards at the next biggest block of time—the blocks. What two or three big things can get done to take the person to their yearlong goal? Those are the block goals.

Within the block there are four programs. The goal of each program will take the person closer to the block goal.

Each program is four weeks long. The action of each week should take the person closer to the program goal.

If this all lines up, it's perfect. The act of just laying it out to give someone something to start with is a beautiful thing. It is likely going to change as the year goes on. As the sage philosopher Mike Tyson once said, "Everyone has a plan until they get punched in the face." Each person will, without a doubt, get punched in the face throughout the course of the year. I mean that 100% metaphorically. Unless you train fighters—they're definitely getting punched in the face.

I'm not sure where I first heard the next clichéd saying that I'm about to lay on you, but it's heavy on the truth side of things:

*Plans never work but planning always does.*

We need a course charted so that we have something to course correct. If we don't we are flying blind.

### Getting it Done

To pull off planning like this, and act on it effectively, people have to consider all of the things they need to work the plan and get it done. Otherwise this all ends up as really nice thoughts on paper. The planning needs some specific action guides to make sure people fit the plan realistically into their lives and carry it out. Here's what we have people consider:

*Schedule:* When are you going to do the actions that take you closer to your goals?

*Resources:* What do you need to get the job done? Do you have all you need? Are there things you need to get to make sure you can do the things you want to do?

*Accountability:* How would you like to be held accountable to your plan? What can we do to help?

*Obstacles:* What could get in the way of your success? There's always something...

*Strategies to Overcome Obstacles:* What will you do to overcome the obstacles should they pop up?

### Remember the Most Important Things

The most important thing is that our people have some sort of vision to act on. Everyone needs an aim to validate their struggles, otherwise it's easy to disregard action. So, while the plan may not be perfect, it needs to exist. It's likely going to change anyway, but we need it to get us going—we can always adjust along the way.

The equally most important thing is that action trumps a well-theorized plan. Things are rarely going to come out of someone's brain perfectly, but if they have enough to act on, and we can course correct along the way, that's great. We just need action and often the goal, or the plan, becomes clearer.

## End of Block Coaching Recap

- Give the person enough time to think and write by giving them the form ahead of time
- Remember that you're still the facilitator
- Ask open-ended questions and reflect answers
- Let them write more if need be
- Use the tools to help them get unstuck
- If necessary, shrink the timeframe

## Aims and Goals in Closing

When a person has a goal, or a series of goals, that he or she truly desires to achieve, action becomes simpler and more purposeful. Life, or at least one corner of it, makes a lot more sense. Most folks, unfortunately, don't have a lot of structured experience with setting, acting towards, and achieving goals. They've been missing out on the clarity and simplicity of a goal-driven existence—and it's especially true in relation to their training and fitness. It's our duty to change that.

That change is first sponsored by our awareness that goal-setting and achieving is a skill—and that we must introduce the process in a way that allows people to build skill. Starting with the least complexity (short time frames and simple actions) and progressing to more complexity (longer time frames and multiple-step actions) gives folks the slow-cooking they need to develop goal-setting and achieving skills. Guide the progression with consistency and structure and clients completely transform the way they think about goals and their abilities to achieve them.

# Part II: Managing the Three Fitness Coaching Environments

Present day, in-person, fitness coaching has three main arenas—personal training, small group personal training, and group training. Different folks practice different iterations of each, but the goal with this section is to lay out how we do things at our gym to give you considerations for how you might adapt or improve what you're currently doing.

As they say in the hollas (that's "hollows" if you prefer proper American English) of Pennsylvania, there's more than one way to skin a buck. But I think we're on to some solid "skinning techniques" that you can learn from and adapt to your setting. In these sections on each coaching environment I give you big considerations to think about not a play by play. Read them, try them out, and then mold them into your own methods.

I'll preface the rest of this chapter by mentioning that our flagship program is small group personal training—the other two are the supporting boats at our facility. That being said, we've focused intently on the structure of all three to give them as much productive and consistent shape as possible...and it all works.

Let's set sail aboard the flagship first and initiate the discussion with small group personal training.

# Small Group Personal Training

Let's begin with a definition:

*Small group personal training is a model that employs individualized fitness programming in a multi-client, and coach, training environment.*

Each client has their own program, but up to eight clients train in our small group personal training program each hour, while we maintain a coach to client ratio of 1:4-5. The environment is seriously autonomous—each client moves freely on their own, it's not just a group session during which folks have individual programs. Outside of coaching and the program, it's nearly 100% self-directed.

## The Main Job of a Small Group Personal Training Coach

There's a mountain worth of tasks to perform while coaching in a small group personal training model, and atop that mountain sits one, the king, and it is called 'managing the environment.' As a small group personal training coach, that's your number one job—to manage the training environment.

Small group personal training relies on client self-direction; that means there are people moving around and essentially doing their own thing—with guidance from their programs and from their coaches. It's productive, the clients learn how to better manage themselves in a gym; and fun, everyone gets to know each other and community is formed. But that also means that there are a lot of moving parts and personalities.

Our job as coach is to be this weird kind of flexible, yet firmly adhesive, glue that gives people the freedom of movement they need while also binding the whole operation together.

## Build Context and Competency on the Front End

People need to feel competent in order to be self-directed. So, even if you run a predominately small group personal training gym, I recommend doing some kind of orientation session, that's mostly one-on-one, on the front end before someone begins their structured program. During this orientation, folks learn how to generally perform the big movements and are introduced to ideas that help them connect with what they are doing. Building context and competency on the front end with an orientation session gives people more freedom to navigate the environment effectively when following their training program—helping them move more quickly toward success and making your job as a coach easier.

For example, during our orientation, new clients learn the warm-up and they also are introduced to the basics of the hinge, squat, upper-push, and upper-pull. One coach will teach them the warm-up in a one-on-one setting, and another coach will walk them through the movement orientation. Sometimes, however, one coach will do the entire orientation. This is usually a case of the gym being busy and us making the decision to limit confusion by limiting changes. No matter the coaching set-up, new clients learn all of the basics that set them up for success during their first small group personal training session.

## Warm-up Engagement

The warm-up is the best place to build the barrier between what's going a person's life outside the gym and the work that they're about to do in the gym. While warm-up coaching may not always be the most technical coaching task, it's the keystone that locks the entire session together.

As people start their warm-ups at BSP NOVA, this is when we GAB with them (refer to the GAB in the section on Aims and Goals). Right away we're shifting focus from the outside world and helping them form their intent for the next hour of their lives. It's also when we get people engaging with each other so that everyone can interact and enjoy their workout. You'd be surprised at how much banter a "would you rather" question starts.

Maybe most importantly, this is our opportunity to chat with each client individually and get a read on where they are for the day—figure out their training readiness and just seeing how in the hell they're doing. It's just a great time for people to feel seen and acknowledged. No one should ever sneak into the first exercise of their warm-up without being chatted up by a coach.

That's all well and good, but how does the warm-up integrate with the rest of the environment and the other skills we need to tie it all together? It's all about flow.

## Build a Flow

Movement through your space needs to make sense—it's best if there are defined areas for different activities. This does a few things for us as managers of the environment.

First—it helps clients sort out the when and where of what they're supposed to do. They have a path to follow, which keeps them from straying too far in any unnecessary direction. And it also keeps psychological strife at bay for them. The environment is ordered, and they know how to navigate it. And, more practically, people are less likely to be tripping all over each other—which is especially important if you're operating in a smallish space.

Second—for us as coaches, it keeps movement somewhat contained throughout the space. Having designated areas for warming up, strength training, and conditioning creates zones (more on these in a hot second) that are easier to manage and limits the need to corral people moving all willy-nilly. We want self-direction, but self-direction must be through an environment that is understandable and navigable.

At BSP NOVA, we have areas designated for warm-up and medicine ball throws, strength training, and conditioning. People move seamlessly through each area as they follow their program and eventually head out the door for the day.

## Zone Coaching

If you're a solo coach in a semi-private environment, this section might not be as important to you, but if you're part of, or running, a system that uses more than one coach at a time in a small group personal training environment, perk up!

At BSP NOVA, our coaches cover zones. If one coach is in the strength zone, the other will be in another zone—unless the situation dictates that two coaches should be in the strength zone. This allows us to spread attention throughout the gym and make sure that nothing important gets missed.

Zone coaching also maintains training as the priority over socializing. There's no doubt that you want a healthy social aspect in the small group personal training setting, but it can't be the highest priority—and it can quickly elevate to the number one spot if some structure isn't in place. Coaches tend to congregate and then clients follow suit, creating a herd of people having a great conversation but not getting a damn thing done—or taking way too long to get done what they need to get done. Spreading things out a bit, combats this.

The zones expand, and contract, based on the time of day and the number of clients. For example, if it's the first time slot of the morning or afternoon, the coaches will both be in the warm-up zone and expand out as clients begin to move into different parts of their workouts. As more clients shuffle in, the zones stay expanded.

Coaches can alternate between zones, they aren't stationed in a zone for an entire shift, but we need the floor covered, so we have to be aware of where the other coach is at all times so that potential issues, and potential celebrations, don't get missed.

This probably sounds super stiff and sterile—it's not. You can manage zone coaching without having a stick in your ass. Our coaches move around, have fun with clients, and talk to each other, but they understand that the floor needs covered so they don't congregate in the same zone for too long.

We do, however, mandate that coaches check in with each other every thirty minutes. That could be a quick convo, or it could be simply crossing each other's face and slapping hands.

### No Backs to Clients/Always be Yellow

In his book *Unbeatable Mind*, Mark Divine uses the phrase "always be yellow" to describe how it's useful to always have your attention on and not get lulled to sleep. We adopted that term for our coaching. Always be yellow, for us, means no backs to clients. As we expand out in our zones we do our best to make sure the only thing to our backs are the walls—unless we are moving in to closely coach someone.

### Understand Space vs. Attention
### (Watch from a distance, close the gap to coach)

Managing the environment means seeing as much of it as you can at one time—a consistent vigil of scanning. That is until you see something that needs addressed and you need to move in for coaching.

We stand back, taking scope of the entire zone we are coaching until we see a coaching point, then we move in to help the person. Being able to take in an entire zone, and scan it, helps us set appropriate priorities about where our attention is most needed at the time. For example, if there's a new client we'll likely need to hang with them more—or if someone is performing a heavy, technical lift we can decide to move in closer to coach.

Seeing the big picture also helps to identify potential problems before they arise and intervene before, well, those problems become problems. Closing the gap to coach allows us to make the instructional environment more intimate and we can personalize the coaching approach to the person. Rarely, if ever, do we coach from farther away than a few feet. There are extenuating circumstances that sometimes require a long-distance cue from across the gym, but we avoid it as much as possible.

## The Paradigm Applies

Once you close the gap, apply the four-part coaching paradigm as it fits with the person you are coaching. (See the paradigm discussion in the Guidance section.)

## Defining Success

It's important to define what success is with any job, but since the small group personal training setting is so open and freely moving, it's even more important to have a clear definition of success. If not, there's a good chance coaches won't have a solid grasp on what just happened during their shift. They also won't have the best idea of how to manage themselves as they coach, manage the environment, and keep it all loosely glued. That's why we have our coaching checklist. It gives a guide for directing our actions and a way to evaluate ourselves each day to know whether or not we were successful—as well as what we have to do to improve.

## What's My Purpose?

In the midst of the moving parts of the small group personal training environment—the conversations, the coaching, the freedom to sit back and watch—it's easy to lose focus and drift off. It's just as easy to get locked in on one person and forget about the rest of the environment. The space and freedom coaches enjoy also cracks the window of the brain so that life from outside the gym may creep in and take over our thoughts. We need a tool to combat that.

Anytime we feel ourselves drifting off, hyper-focusing on one person, or generally feeling amiss, we ask ourselves *what's my purpose right now?*

The purpose is to coach, create an incredible training environment, and help people progress.

When you feel yourself drifting, snap yourself back in with that question.

*What's my purpose right now?*

P.S. It works for pretty much every situation in work and in life, not just small group personal training.

## Small Group Personal Training in Closing

That's the general outline that we follow for success as a small group personal training coach. Understanding, first, that we are environment managers makes the big picture of small group personal training easier to grasp. Managing the environment from a group, social level down to an individual level requires skill derived from consistency and structure. Remember, consider all of this within the context of your environment and apply with your situation in mind.

# One-on-One Personal Training

One-on-one training is likely the best experience lender that a fitness coach can borrow from to improve and expand their coaching repertoire. It's also pretty damn weird—and by weird I mean polarizing. People tend to either love it or hate it. And it can be super productive or devolve into a dancing monkey show with the trainer counting reps and entertaining the client rather than guiding the person toward success. It takes a lot of focus, energy, and giving—and that is draining work.

But, as I said in the first sentence, it's a great way to gain experience. I sincerely believe that it's something every fitness coach should do at some point in their career. I've done a lot of it in mine, and I'm going to share what I've learned that makes sessions successful and keeps you from burning yourself to the ground like a redneck's fireworks shack on Fourth of July.

## Program as Far in Advance as Possible

With most personal training clients buying session packages, and not thinking in terms of programming, it's easy to get caught up in the game of just writing workouts for a given day. Why write a long-term program when you're only guaranteed ten sessions, right? That's a valid question. But only planning for those ten sessions isn't the best thing to do for you or for the client.

Results take time and effort, and we need to make sure we're clear with clients and communicate that with them up front. Writing a program for four to six weeks is a simple action that lets people know that ten sessions probably isn't going to do it. (Unless they hired you for some short-term reason like cleaning up their lifting form.) If it's a new client, it shows them that you're already thinking about helping them long-term and that you care about their success. That's a good thing for them to know.

Besides communicating that commitment to the long-term is the way to go, having a program ready for your clients that goes beyond their scheduled sessions makes your life a lot easier. Trying to figure out what you're going to do with someone "as you go" is a miserable, anxiety-provoking feeling. Working from a written program saves you that strife.

Also, it's much easier to adapt an existing plan than it is to try to come up with a new one every week, or heaven forbid, every session. If you program out for all of your clients at least month in advance, even if they haven't committed to that long of a term yet, you'll save yourself a lot of work and worry in the long run.

Think about that cumulatively. Let's, for consideration's sake, say that you have ten one-on-one clients. And for each of those clients you try to come up with a new workout for each session—and you train each of those clients twice per week. That's twenty times that you'll have to work and worry throughout the course of the week. But if you write a month-long program for each of them, that's only ten times per month that you have to put a plan together.

Program out for you clients as far in advance as you can—usually four to six weeks. If they're new, they'll see that you value you them enough to plan ahead for them and you communicate the importance of long-term training. You'll also save yourself a bunch of time, work, and worry.

## Control as Much as You Can Control

Most folks with a steady stream of one-on-one's work in the commercial gym setting—meaning that there is a ton of shit going on all around you at all times, exposing you and your clients to a lot of variables that you can't control. There are creepy guys that make sex-moans as they foam roll, old ladies that are far more aggressive than appropriate with the inny-outy machine (you know which one I'm talking about), and the ever-present jagaloon that commandeers a bench for forty-five minutes so he can talk on the phone to his boo-thang about the workout that he isn't doing.

It's a circus sometimes.

To keep that circus from pitching its big top over your session, create a "micro-environment" for your client and yourself.

Here's what to do:

Set up as much equipment as you can in advance. That's really it.

If you know someone is going to start with kettlebell swings and core work, have that laid out for them. Then, if you're able to work the next step ahead, and know that they'll be barbell deadlifting after those swings, commandeer a bar and get it set up. Get everything you need to train your client for the duration of the session and contain it in a little nook of the gym—that way you can watch the circus, but you don't have to be part of the show.

This pre-session set up does a few things for us.

First, it makes the session way more efficient—and more efficiency means more density. That, in turn, means a better chance for your client to get results because they're able to fit in more work.

Second, it conserves energy and focus. Having a controlled environment for your session creates a nice little safe haven for your client to "relax" in. That buffer, that seemingly sane corner of control, decreases the need to be constantly scanning the environment for what's going on around them, who's close, who isn't, etc. It also just limits the amount each of you has to think about how to make the session work—hunting down equipment, securing space, etc.

I know this sounds hunky dory and you might be thinking that there is no way in hell that it will work in your environment. I'm not saying that it's easy, or that it's always going to work perfectly, but it's worth making every effort to make it happen.

Find some space. Set up the equipment you need for your next client's program. Guard that area. Watch your session go super smoothly.

## G.A.B. Before the Session Starts

Being a one-on-one coach gives you the opportunity to set a strong intent with every client during every session. That's a wonderful thing.

Before getting cracking on the session, as you're checking in on the human in front of you, get a GAB session in and set a goal for the day. Both of you will be more intently focused for the next hour and there's less of a chance of it turning into a therapy session. (More on that in a bit).

See the GAB discussion in the Guidance section for a refresher on how to get it done.

## Walk Them Through the Session Before the Session Starts

After/during your GAB session, walk the client through everything that's going to happen for the day. Pull out your handy-dandy program that you've already written (hint, hint, wink, wink) and show/remind them of the exercises they'll be doing for the day. Point out what they did last week, or last session, and let them conceptualize the session with the visual of the program. This will keep them from wasting energy on wondering what is about to happen, they can focus in on training because they have the path they have to navigate in their brain.

As a bonus, this is a great opportunity for them to acknowledge and reflect on progress. They'll get to see what they did last week, see some incremental steps forward, and get focused for what they'll do with the next hour of their lives.

## The Coaching/Convo Happy Medium

Your clients are partly paying for conversation, so you can't deny them it. But it's draining on you, and unproductive for them, if your entire session turns into a talkfest. Walking them through the session before it starts, and GABing to set an intent, helps keep focus. Other ways to keep the session moving are to stick to rest periods. In our small group personal training we don't worry so much about that, but in a private coaching environment where the chat monster can flap its chatty gums at any minute, rest periods keep people moving. Actually, just physically moving helps keep the chat monster in the depths as well. It locks pace and urgency into the session. So, pair exercises together, keep at least semi-strict rest periods, and keep moving between the exercises and you can keep the convo at a happy medium.

## Manage Your Energy

Up to this point, we've discussed conducting the session in a way that's productive. For this section, which will be a bit longer and include some subsections, we're talking about managing ourselves so that we can be who we need to be for our clients and avoid burning ourselves out.

### *Focus on Your Mindset*

Let's start with some gratitude. You help other people exercise, and they pay you money for it. I'm not trying to be preachy, but sometimes we have to remind ourselves of that. Let it sink in for a minute (because you could be sinking knee deep into shit that you have to clean up right now and getting paid minimum wage for it.)

Beyond taking some time for gratitude, and writing down some things that you're generally grateful for in a journal, develop a system for yourself to keep your head on straight.

At the most basic level, just make some time for yourself that you know is just yours—and don't give it up for anything. Seriously, be like a rabid raccoon that found a cocaine stash every time someone, or something, tries to take that time away from you.

Also, be consistent with something. Have something that you just check the box on every day. That consistency will give your psyche some bedrock. It could be as simple as making your bed every day. Just have something that absolutely gets done every day without negotiation.

If you're grateful, make some time for yourself, and stay consistent with at least one thing every day, you'll have a better chance of keeping your head in a good place.

## *Stack Your Sessions*

Do your best to stack your sessions by scheduling them back-to-back with a small break for set-up in between. I understand that this is perfect world kind of stuff, especially accounting for the small break, but if you can sort this out to be at least close to optimal, you'll be in way better shape energy wise. Rather than having a bunch of rises and falls throughout the day, you get a solid block of work with a longer refractory period that you can use to play and recover.

Also, stacking your sessions makes you look busy. Looking busy is good. You appear exclusive and valuable—which is true.

### *Keep Tabs on Personalities*

Why people and How people can be especially draining clients. They often need a lot of conversation. They
just need a lot out of you, and you have to keep that in mind as you roll into and out of sessions. Be conscious of where your head is at before you go into a session. If you know someone is going to take a lot out of you, focus on keeping a boundary between you and the client while still serving them and giving them what they
need. It also helps to frame your thoughts with some unconditional positive regard before starting the session, and remember that, you're both human beings and you each are a little weird.

Take your breaks after those challenging folks so you don't carry that juju into the next session, and so you have time to recover and get your mind right before helping the next person.

## Get Out of the Gym

Seriously, at least once per day, get out of the gym. I don't even care what you do, unless it's some kind of Russian espionage or you go to a baby seal punting convention—I do mind those things. Just get out of there and get some space. Don't get bullied into thinking that you have to be there every working minute of the day.

## Build a Community Around Yourself

This section is about your longevity and long-term success—and also about connecting people to other people so that they can help take care of each other. Let's talk about two things that you can do to build a community around yourself.

### *Introduce Your Clients to Each Other*

Connecting your clients builds a supportive web that helps them hold each other up. As you pass from one client to the next, have the one departing hang back for a second, if they have some time, to meet the person about to start. Create a Facebook group that connects all of your clients. Sponsor some happy hours that get everyone together. While you're doing this, facilitate a conversation between them all so they get to know each other, they start to care about each other, and they continue to help each other kick ass.

## Introduce Your Clients to Your Fellow Trainers

No one wants to be around the insecure, wary person. People want to be around the confident sharer and connector. That's what a true alpha personality is—the person that leads from the front and protects while also connecting people, sharing, and making people feel welcome. They don't hide in scarcity and insecurity. If you want your clients to view you as that type of person—the confident connector and protector—introduce them to other trainers in your gym. Make them see how you understand your own value and you lead from the front by being a team member. Make them feel comfortable by showing them around to the other people inhabiting their space.

## One-on-One in Conclusion

One-one-one training is a great way for coaches to learn a lot about people and how to communicate—and it's also a great way for us to have a huge, individual impact. This section offers you a lot to consider as a one-on-one coach. If it all seems overwhelming, start with one thing from this discussion and implement that into your one-on-one practice, work on it for a few weeks, and then add in another piece. And, remember, there's a solution in here that fits your context, you just have to think, apply, observe, and then modify.

# Group Training

Group training is a lot of fun, and it's also a great lower-cost option for folks that can't afford the higher-end services like small group personal training and one-on-one training. The caveat is that group training, to be done safely and successfully, needs a solid framework and structure. It also requires a different coaching energy that the other two types of training don't necessitate. I'm not saying you have to be Richard Simons, but some you need some presence so that the room doesn't fall flat.

During this dive into group training we'll cover the structure, function, and flair (cue jazz hands!) that defines a great group-training program. Before we go any further, keep in mind that we're discussing the BSP NOVA brand of group training. We run a "strength camp" type class with a semi-individualized training template and a metabolic conditioning class. It's also important to mention that no more than twelve clients can schedule for a given class—and we know who is scheduled before class starts. With that in mind, let's continue.

We'll begin with the initial eval.

# The Evaluation

For our group classes, we use a simple movement evaluation.

For the shoulders we use the Apley's scratch test and a shoulder CAR.

For the hips we do an active straight leg raise.

We also do a trunk stability push-up.

In our strength training classes, we place people into either the hips or shoulders group, and the get a wrist band to denote which group they're in, and we format their programming options to fit the group.

Metabolic isn't as structured. We just use the information to help our coaches guide the clients through the varying levels of exercise difficulty that they can choose from.

Basic info is necessary to make sure we don't put people in terrible positions. There's no programming customization, so we don't have to go as deep with a movement eval.

# First Thing's First—Format

Here's the exact document we use with our coaches to guide our group sessions:

### *Beginning of the session/pre-game:*

- *Call everyone together to get started exactly on time*
- *The Pre-game Pow-Wow*
    - *Announcements*
    - *What's happening today?*
    - *Goal:*
        - *Ask what individual goal(s) each person wants to set for themselves today*

### *Session:*

- *Warm-up*
- *Huddle*
    - *Cues*
    - *Things to think about during main exercises*
    - *How to do main exercises*
- *Do main training segment*

- *Huddle*
  - *Cues*
  - *Things to think about during next training segment*
  - *How to do next exercises*
- *Do second exercise block*
- *Huddle*
  - *Cues*
  - *Things to think about during finisher*
  - *How to do finisher*

**Cool-Down**

- *Do cool down exercises*
- *Huddle*
  - *Check in on individual goals*
  - *Announcements*
  - *Do a team "breakdown" on something ridiculous*

This structure was born from my time playing, and coaching, football—minus some of the continual goal-setting stuff. Each time we'd work on something at our individual positions, or collectively as a defense (I played safety/linebacker in college), we'd huddle up, get instructions, then break out again to act. It kept everything orderly, built rest into the practice, and gave us the ability to shift focus and reorient it on the next task.

It applies nicely to all group-training sessions—folks need rest, they need attention breaks, and they need a chance to re-focus before heading into the next segment of the workout. This pause for instruction is also huge for putting people in the best possible positions to be successful—more on that in just a tick.

I added in the goal setting part of the process during the past year. We GAB for our small group personal training and one-on-one sessions; why would we sell our group-training clients short on that beautiful opportunity to focus their intent over the next immediate time block of their lives?

Having a structure like this, and sticking to it consistently, makes the process of teaching class, as well as progressing it, much less stressful on you. And it makes it easier for the clients to understand, focus, train hard, and make progress.

## Instructing—The Whole Group

Rather than attempting to coach everything on the fly, as people are whizzing about in the class, use those breaks in the format wisely and give people the information they need to be successful. It sets context, it gives people the cues for them to keep in mind as they act, and it gives them the information they need to make the right exercise selection.

Our programming for our group classes is also instructive—we use a one-up, one-down system. You can see that in the pictures below.

We give a solid demonstration, associated cues, and big things to think about.

During the instruction period we give folks information that help them make the right exercise choice for them. This is true for our group strength classes as well, but each person in the strength classes carries their own programming sheet instead of having the class written on a chalkboard. It's like small group personal training lite.

Also, give everyone reminders and bring up salient issues from past classes. When I say that, I mean talk about them as themes, don't call out person specific actions. State it like:

> "Something to keep in mind about X..."

Not like:

> "I noticed last class that Debbie had a hard time with X, so..." or "Hey, here's something everyone keeps messing up..."

That's not to be overly sensitive, it's just not the best way to get everyone on board and learning.

As you move through each section of the class, you're going to notice thematic coaching points, things that more than one person seems to struggle with, and also things that only one person is struggling with. You'll, of course, deal with those in real time, but it's also helpful to bring them up during breaks and include them in the group instruction.

Here's a helpful way to frame that:

*Individual issue, Group instruction*

Again, a great way to state it is, *"Hey ladies and gents, here's something to keep in mind about X..."*

Adding this in to group instruction time gives everyone the benefit of learning from the mistakes of one or a few.

## A Little More on One-up, One-down: Qualifications

Have you ever been teaching a class and had folks doing exercises at varying levels of difficulty? Say, a couple people are swinging kettlebells while a couple more are relegated to a lower-level hip hinge? Of those folks doing the lower-level hinge, one or more is bound to wonder, and eventually ask why they aren't doing swings, too, with an envious, sometimes resentful air. You know, with one of those poopy looks on their face with their nose all scrunched up.

Well, here's something you can do about that—have everyone run through qualifications each time to reinforce the progression and that they are being put in the best position to be successful.

**If you can do this, then you get to do that.**

For example, let's look at the kettlebell swing.

Have everyone demonstrate a belly swing. Nailed it? Cool. Move on.

Then a kettlebell RDL. Good? Ok, next step.

How about a kettlebell deadlift? Good? Moving on!

The hike? How's that looking? Solid. Great.

Dead stop swing? Splendid. You're good to go for swings.

If people break down at any level, that's where they hang out—or they do an exercise that would stress them appropriately that would be a lateralization from a kettlebell swing. For example, we have people do vertical jumps instead of swings if they can't demonstrate all of the necessary swinging prerequisites.

You can do this for every complex exercise in your group programming. This may seem like a long process, but it can literally be done in a minute or two. Another reason that the breaks built into the structure are so important.

## Individual Instruction: Crossing Faces

If you take a gander back up at our class guide, you'll see this line:

*Cross face at as many stations during each round as possible*

That's a gentle reminder to keep moving during class. Even though it's a group class, we want as much individual interaction as possible. At a base level, this keeps people connected. From a movement coaching perspective, it gives us the chance to see, and correct, more potential issues—or reinforce the good things that we are seeing.

As you move about, clean up the little issues that you can and take mental notes to check in on them during the break. It's important to think in terms of priorities. You aren't going to get to everything, even though everything may seem important. So, you have to set a hierarchy in your mind that looks something like this:

- Dangerous shit gets attention first

- Then potentially dangerous shit
- Then form flaws that could cumulatively lead to dangerous shit
- Then little tweaks

If you don't have a hierarchy like this, you're going to try to fix everything all of the time as you do your individual coaching and you're going to get really frustrated because that's super hard to do. Or you're going to slow the pace of class so much that people get pissed off. Construct your hierarchy and follow it.

In the case that there's nothing to coach with a given person, still cross their face and engage them in some way during each round—if possible. It's tough if you're working with super short intervals—but make your best effort.

Engage! Engage! Engage!

## What About the Basics?

How in the name everything holy can we get people practicing good exercise execution before they hit the group class running? It's a lot simpler than you think. We use the warm-up.

Each day during the warm-up the basic movement patterns are reinforced and taught—especially for the hinge and squat. This gives us a chance to teach new comers without having to do an entire on-boarding or orientation class, and it's a constant reinforcement for class vets.

Build practice into the warm-up and you can ensure that people are nailing the basics before jumping into loaded, or intensely executed, movements. This is also a great extension of the evaluation—you get to consistently see where someone's movement is progressing, regressing, or stagnating. That's gold for coaching and programming—even in the group setting.

## Firm, But Fun

Group training is centered on fun, graded exercise—that means group classes need to have energy; lots of folks join group training because they like the environment, the shared struggle, the cooperative competition. Being a stick in the mud without any personality will Johnny Raincloud that environment into submission in a hurry. But being overly firm produces the same result.

It's about being firm but fun.

Stated simply, that means preparing yourself as much as possible so that you can be confident in your coaching and in the execution of the class. If there are any holes in your preparation, they will show through, and you won't be as confident as you need to be to be a presence and manage the environment. That means use your grownup voice when addressing everyone.

Project. Stand tall. Move. Be a presence. Demonstrate that you have command over the situation.

This all comes from preparation—both in understanding the class and what should happen, but also in getting your head to the right place before getting rolling.

But class needs to be fun, too. That's why we play a game after each warm-up during metabolic class and we end each Friday strength class with a game. Beyond the games, however, you need to be fun. While everyone will feed off of the energy of the others in the class, your energy sets the tone. If you're not enjoying yourself, no one else will have as much fun as they should. (Maybe that's not true. Lots of folks have fun regardless, but you know what I'm getting at.)

## Group Training in Conclusion

Develop a structure that allows you to prepare, teach, and program consistently for your group classes—that way you can instruct effectively and be relaxed enough to create a firm but fun environment. It's truly that simple.

## The Big Three in Conclusion

I mentioned in the intro to this section that small group personal training is our flagship program...we love it and have seen it guide people to dramatic physical, mental, and emotional transformations. I'd hazard to say we think it's the best way to train people. But that's just us in our little never-never land, getting to do whatever we want all the time because we make up the rules in our own gym. You might not be in the same situation. Maybe you work at a commercial gym and have to train people one-on-one. Perhaps you're at a studio that does only group training. No worries, baby, that's cool.

The main consideration, that is the mothership of all the considerations I laid out during each section, is that you're doing your absolute best to create a consistent, structured environment for whatever type of fitness coaching you're employing. What can you do to control the things that you can control? That's the most important question to answer. Between your own experience, and the considerations laid out for you in this chapter, you have the answers.

I'll actually leave you with one more parting thought on this...on the answers. One of the answers is to realize you're never done building and tweaking. The best coaching systems are consistent, but they're also consistently evolving. So, add new rungs to your scaffolding as you keep the basic structure intact.

Then you'll be able to keep giving your clients better paths for climbing and simpler ways to guide them.

## Concluding Thoughts

I guess we could call this the epilogue. It's my attempt to tie this coaching escapade together and allow you to part from this experience with cohesive understanding about what just happened...and maybe a little of what to do about what just happened. I won't keep you long, scouts honor.

Thematically, what I hope you've realized is that fitness coaching is a dynamic sumbitch. There are so many elements that interact in so many ways to construct just what it is that we do for a living. It's the mindfulness of that dynamic sumbitch, and how multi-dimensional it is that allows us to be good at, and to continue to improve at, fitness coaching. It's an understanding that we are never done, and it's incredibly liberating once you accept it. Hopefully, though, it's not something you just have to accept. Hopefully it's your innate and insatiable curiosity that drives you to explore all of these multi-dimensional, dynamic elements in far greater detail than I could express in this book.

We've explored some of what makes the folks that we coach tick and their general reasons for seeking us out. I took a lot of information, experience, and knowledge and condensed it into something as applicable, and thought provoking, as I possibly could. Like my mom always asked me to do (we call her Hot Kath), I did my best.

People, however, are outrageously complex. Maybe the most complex things in the known universe. So, many aspects of our species, especially those that guide just why in the hell we do the things we do, will forever be somewhat mysterious. And I think that's kind of cool. The information that I have been able to share comes from my insatiable curiosity about people and the choices they make...and why they make those choices. If we want to be great at this job, and stick around doing it well for a long time, that insatiable curiosity is a pre-req. The X's and O's of programming and coaching exercises are absolute necessities to nail. But it's the curiosity and love of people that will keep you in this game, changing lives and creating a life for yourself as you do it.

As we consider that fitness coaching is dynamic and that we need to be insatiable curious about people, we also have to consider what we are going to do to act on that knowledge. I'm positive that you came to this book with a toolbox full of great...well...tools that have helped you help folks of all creeds and abilities. Consider, always, what you can do to make them better—to make the toolbox bigger or to sharpen and enhance the tools that lie inside it. I mentioned several times throughout this book that you should take this work apply it, challenge it, expand your toolbox, examine what elements work for you, and discard those that don't.

With all that said, there is a wealth of time and experience tested info in here that is ripe for use in the betterment of other folks' lives. Act on it. Please, don't just read and then be done. Act, in one way or the other, on the info that you found in this book. Anyone can read and then decide they know, but it takes another type of person to read and then do. The doing is where the real knowledge comes from. The doing is what's most important.

I hope you've enjoyed yourself and found these discussions useful. Thanks so much for sharing your time with me.

# Acknowledgements

Chris Merritt...thank you for your unshakeable support, your friendship, and your ability to keep me on the straight and narrow. Your trust in me to help you make Beyond Strength Performance NOVA into a world-class training facility has given me the license to grow personally and professionally in ways that I otherwise wouldn't have been able to. Most of what is in this book comes from the opportunities that you've given me to experiment and teach. Thank you.

Mike Connelly...over a thousand conversations you've challenged me, supported me, helped me grow, and become a brother. You've given me cause to believe in myself when my confidence waivered, and you've made me laugh my ass off just when I needed it. Thank you.

Bill Hartman...your friendship and mentorship over the past few years, and your push for me to get this book done, has been a beacon guiding me toward a better version of myself. Thank you.

Andy McCloy...thanks for the hundreds of phone conversations that have lead us to become friends.

You've always lent me an ear when I needed it and I hope I've reciprocated as well as I could have. I appreciate your realness. You're a shining beacon to the industry, and to folks in all industries, on what a person can do to transform their life.

BSP NOVA Coaches (Tommy, Greg, Pavlos, Jon, Geoff, Kenny)...you've all given me the opportunity to put the principles in this book into practice, and you've influenced them much more than you know. You've all trusted me to put you in the best positions to be successful in your career and to help you grow personally and professionally. That means a great deal to me. Thank you.

Hot Kath...once again, thanks for keeping me out of that ditch. Your work ethic, and your determination to give me the best life I could possibly have, has influenced me more profoundly than I could ever express to you. I love you, mom, thank you.

# About the Author

Todd Bumgardner is the CEO of Strength Faction and the COO and Director of Staff Development at Beyond Strength Performance NOVA in Sterling, Virginia, as well as a performance consultant for a full-time, Federal, tactical law enforcement unit. He travels broadly to teach coaching workshops and consult with other coaches on how they can improve their coaching skills. He is an avid hunter, and writer, fly fisherman, and musician. Todd splits his time between Northern Virginia and Central Pennsylvania.

Made in the USA
Monee, IL
01 March 2020